Taking Your Android Tablets to the Max

Russell Holly

Apress®

Taking Your Android Tablets to the Max

ISBN-13 (pbk): 978-1-4302-3689-4

ISBN-13 (electronic): 978-1-4302-3690-0

President and Publisher: Paul Manning
Lead Editor: Steve Anglin
Technical Reviewer: Aaron Kasten
Editorial Board: Steve Anglin, Ewan Buckingham, Gary Cornell, Louise Corrigan, Morgan Ertel, Jonathan Gennick, Jonathan Hassell, Robert Hutchinson, Michelle Lowman, James Markham, Matthew Moodie, Jeff Olson, Jeffrey Pepper, Douglas Pundick, Ben Renow-Clarke, Dominic Shakeshaft, Gwenan Spearing, Matt Wade, Tom Welsh
Coordinating Editor: Jessica Belanger
Copy Editor: Kim Wimpsett
Compositor: MacPS, LLC
Indexer: SPi Global
Artist: SPi Global
Cover Designer: Anna Ishchenko

Distributed to the book trade worldwide by Springer Science+Business Media New York, 233 Spring Street, 6th Floor, New York, NY 10013. Phone 1-800-SPRINGER, fax (201) 348-4505, e-mail orders-ny@springer-sbm.com, or visit www.springeronline.com.

For information on translations, please e-mail rights@apress.com, or visit www.apress.com.

Apress and friends of ED books may be purchased in bulk for academic, corporate, or promotional use. eBook versions and licenses are also available for most titles. For more information, reference our Special Bulk Sales–eBook Licensing web page at www.apress.com/bulk-sales.

Contents at a Glance

Contents.. iv

About the Author.. viii

About the Technical Reviewer ix

Introduction x

Chapter 1: Why Android? Which Android? 1

Chapter 2: Choosing the Right Tablet.. 25

Chapter 3: Creating Your Google Account 37

Chapter 4: Taking Advantage of Google Apps 49

Chapter 5: The Play Store 71

Chapter 6: Using the Camera 89

Chapter 7: Music, Movies, and Games 99

Chapter 8: Using Your Android Tablet Wherever You Go............... 121

Chapter 9: Using Your Tablet at Work 133

Chapter 10: Harnessing "the Cloud" on Your Tablet 145

Chapter 11: Customizing Your Android Tablet 155

Chapter 12: Rooting Your Tablet 167

Chapter 13: Using Amazon Apps 177

Index 189

Contents

Contents at a Glance iii

About the Author viii

About the Technical Reviewer ix

Introduction x

Chapter 1: Why Android? Which Android? 1

Android: A Brief History 2

The Open Handset Alliance 2

The T-Mobile G1 5

The Motorola Droid 5

The Google Nexus One 6

The iPad 7

Which Android Tablet Is for Me? 8

Screen Type 9

Screen Size 10

Internet Access 10

Understanding Android User Interface Options 12

HTC Sense 13

Samsung TouchWiz 16

Amazon Kindle Fire 17

Stock Android 3.0 (Honeycomb) 18

Android 4.0 "Ice Cream Sandwich" 21

The Android "Budget Tablet" Without Google 23

Summary 23

Chapter 2: Choosing the Right Tablet 25

Features 25

Size 25

Cameras 26

Memory 26

Internet 27

What Kind of User Are You? 27

A Road Warrior 27

A Tech Gearhead 28

A Student or Teacher 28

A Music and Movie Junkie 28

A Bookworm 28

A Mobile Office User 29

Where Should You Buy Your Tablet? 29

Warranty or Insurance? 30

Accessories? 30

Unboxing Your Tablet 31

Setting Up Your Tablet 32

First Charge 33

Additional Ports 34

SIM Card 34

Powering Up 35

Summary 35

▓ **Chapter 3: Creating Your Google Account** **37**

Creating a Google Account from Your Tablet 38

Creating an Account on Google.com 40

Syncing with Your Google Account 42

Adding Contacts 44

Importing Contacts 45

Adding Contacts Manually 46

Summary 48

▓ **Chapter 4: Taking Advantage of Google Apps** **49**

Gmail 49

Navigate Gmail 50

Compose an E-mail 51

Customize Gmail 53

Google Talk 55

Add Some Friends 56

Set Your Status Message 57

Chat with a Friend 57

Video Chat with a Friend 57

Customize Your Settings 58

Google Maps 59

Find Locations on a Map 60

Add Map Info with Layers 60

Get Directions 62

Find Your Way with Navigation 63

Locate Friends with Latitude 63

YouTube 64

Check Out the Wall 65

Store Videos 66

Share Videos 67

Search 67

Search Your Tablet with the Keypad 68

Search Your Tablet with Spoken Words 68

Summary 69

■Chapter 5: The Play Store 71

Finding and Using Android Apps 71

Choosing an App 73

Installing an App 75

Updating an App 77

Submit a Review 78

Using the Play Store on the Web 79

Using Play Books 80

Using Play Movies 83

Using Google Play Music 86

Summary 88

■Chapter 6: Using the Camera 89

Introducing the Android Camera Apps 89

Using the Tablet Camera 90

Choosing Camera Settings 90

Taking a Photo 92

Recording Video 92

Photographing or Recording Yourself 93

Using the Gallery 93

Grid View 93

Single-Item View 94

Using Other Apps 95

Summary 97

■Chapter 7: Music, Movies, and Games 99

Listening to Music on Your Tablet 99

Playing Stored Music 100

Using Other Music Apps 105

Watching Movies on Your Tablet 109

Watching Stored Movies on Your Tablet 110

Watching Streamed Movies on Your Tablet 111

Playing Games on Your Tablet 117

Finding Games 117

Adding a Controller 119

Summary 120

■Chapter 8: Using Your Android Tablet Wherever You Go 121

Making Your Tablet More Like Your Desktop 121

Sync Your Tablet with Google Chrome 122

Sync Your Tablet with Your Phone 123

Store Files in the Cloud with Dropbox 126

Augmenting Your Reality 128

Navigate the Night Sky with Google Sky Map 128

Learn More About a Location with Layar 130

Summary 132

■Chapter 9: Using Your Tablet at Work 133

Securing Your Tablet 133

Locking Your Screen 133

Letting Others Know You're the Owner (and How to Contact You) 135

Securing Your Google Account 136
Encrypting Stored Information 139
Securing Your Proprietary Network Connections...140
Installing a Security Certificate...140
Protecting Your Certificate with a Password 141
Empowering Your System Administrator 142
Summary 143

■ **Chapter 10: Harnessing "the Cloud" on Your Tablet 145**
Storing Your Data in the Cloud..145
Storing Data with SugarSync...145
Managing Word Documents with Google Docs 148
Computing with Cloud-Provided Services...148
Searching for Images with Google Goggles 149
Accessing Your Home Data Storage with Wyse PocketCloud....................151
Speeding Up Internet Browsing with Opera Mini Browser.........................153
Summary 154

■ **Chapter 11: Customizing Your Android Tablet 155**
Customizing the Keyboard 155
Putting the Keyboard Within Reach of Your Thumbs 155
Accepting Handwritten and Voice Input...158
Customizing Your Home Screen 160
Summary 165

■ **Chapter 12: Rooting Your Tablet 167**
Getting Permission to Root 167
XDA-Developers 168
RootzWiki.com 168
Getting the Most from a Rooted Tablet..168
Exploring the Files on Your Android with Terminal.....................................169
Backing Up Your Device or Apps..170
Taking a Screenshot 173
Summary 175

■ **Chapter 13: Using Amazon Apps 177**
Using the Amazon App Store 178
Installing the Amazon App Store...178
Navigating the App Store 179
Installing App Updates 182
Using the Kindle App...183
Installing the Kindle App 183
Reading in the Kindle App...184
Using the Amazon Video Store..185
Summary 188

Index 189

About the Author

Russell Holly has worked across the IT industry for the last 10 years, gaining experience in server administration, networking, and mobile products. This experience has propelled him into journalism, where he is now considered one of the most knowledgeable in his field on the topic of Android. Russell uses this knowledge to educate and inform in as many places as he can find.

When he's not out looking for the next gadget, Russell works from home with his three children and his wife, Cassandra.

About the Technical Reviewer

Aaron Kasten served as a small and medium business IT consultant for the past 10 years in Texas. In 2008, after a year of planning, Aaron launched AndroidSWAG, an online merchandise company for Android enthusiasts. He also organizes the largest gathering of Android fans and developers, the Big Android BBQ, every October in Texas. He is currently using an HTC Sensation and Samsung Galaxy Tab 10.1.

When not providing IT support or playing with the latest gadgets and phones, Aaron enjoys spending time with family and friends and traveling. He lives in North Texas with his wife and five-pound Chihuahua, Ali.

Introduction

Silently, and without warning, the Android operating system has quickly dominated the mobile ecosystem. This operating system exists in many forms, across many devices, and offers a rich selection of powerful features that could completely change how you accomplish tasks throughout your day. If you're looking for a tablet or have already purchased a tablet, this book will help you navigate through the new world of Android.

Who This Book Is For

If you are reading this book, the chances are good that either you've just gotten an Android tablet or you are hoping to pick the right one for you. You may not be absolutely sure of what the potential of this tablet is or exactly how useful it can be. This book is for users of every skill level to be able to get the most out of any Android tablet.

How This Book Is Structured

This book covers the basics of using an Android tablet, more advanced tricks, and how to modify the look and feel of your tablet.

You'll start off by mastering the basics of navigating your tablet and learning about the benefits of a Google account. Once you've gotten the tablet set up, the book takes you through the different kinds of tasks you are likely to want to accomplish on your tablet, such as sending an e-mail or starting a video chat. Next, you will travel across the Google and Amazon apps that allow you to watch movies, listen to music, and install applications written by developers all around the world.

By the end of the book, you will have the tools necessary to make your tablet a mobile office, a portable home theater system, or the biggest library of books in the world. You'll be able to customize the experience to your personal tastes, and if you're brave enough, you'll be able to try your hand at more serious modifications.

Contacting the Author

Should you have any questions or comments—or even spot a mistake you think we should know about—you can contact the author at thatrussellholly@gmail.com.

Why Android? Which Android?

If you are picking up this book, there stands a good chance you have heard of Android before, and well you should. To see the explosive growth of the Android operating system since it was released, despite never really becoming a household name, is significant. To know that in such a short time Android has surpassed Apple's iOS, on devices like the iPhone and iPad, is more than remarkable. So, yes, you have likely heard of Android. Maybe you've heard of it as a "Droid" or as a Samsung, Motorola, or HTC. You are probably looking for a way to incorporate Android into your daily life. Maybe you are tired of lugging your big laptop everywhere you go. Maybe your smartphone screen is just too small to do everything you need it to do. Reading e-mail, browsing the Web, whatever you may be doing—you've decided it might be time for a tablet.

Android tablets do not fit a specific form factor, personality type, or general purpose. There is an Android tablet out there for every kind of person. When you are given an Android tablet, you are given a blank slate with nearly unlimited potential. Your Android tablet can be as complicated or as simple as you choose it to be. An Android tablet can be little more than a storage device for your library of books, or it can be your mobile command center for holding web conferences, playing video games, or even gazing at the stars. When choosing to buy a tablet, you choose an Android tablet because it's the device for you.

This book will offer you a top-to-bottom guide to choosing one of the many Android tablets. You will get some help in choosing which device would be best for you, take a look at the best apps for your needs, and even spend some time optimizing your tablet to get the most out of it. *Taking Your Android Tablet to the Max!* is written for every kind of person interested in an Android tablet. It doesn't matter if you are a tech god, a college student, a soccer mom, or a business professional, this book will help you make an educated decision and get the most out of your next device.

Taking Your Android Tablet to the Max! covers everything from selecting the device that is best for you to offering maintenance tricks, preserving the battery life, and making sure your tablet lasts. We'll go into the depths of "rooting" your Android tablet and how to not only enable new and exciting features but get the tools you need to make sure your Android tablet is always on the bleeding edge of the latest and greatest from Google. We'll include brief tutorials on utilizing Google's developer tools and show you everything you will need to make sure all your friends, co-workers, and neighbors will be ready to go get one for themselves. Add *Taking Your Android Tablet to the Max!* to your bookshelf, and get ready to get the most out of your tablet.

Android: A Brief History

Everyone knows Android as "the Google OS," but that's not entirely true. Android, Inc., was once its own company, and Android was its brainchild. In 2003, the startup had a plan to create a smarter phone that was aware of a user's location and preferences. At the time, it was something that technology simply wasn't doing, though today location-based services are a global trend.

Android is a perfect example of what happens when innovators put their heads together. As a small startup, however, Android realized it would be much slower in getting its change to the world. The company needed a powerful catalyst. We can think of no company that is better at taking unique ideas and putting them into daily use than Google. In 2005, when Android, Inc., was only 22 months old, it was bought by Google. Google was not quite ready to launch something to the masses. There was a bigger plan in the works, something that would require the resources of many companies in order to solve some of the more fundamental problems in the phone world.

The Open Handset Alliance

The cell phone world was kind of a mess in 2005. Every cell phone manufacturer had a different plug to charge their phones, and most of them would change with the release of a new device from that manufacturer. The must-have feature on a phone was a camera, and e-mail was a feature that most did not have. If there was extra content to be had on your device, it was controlled by the carrier. Ringtones, wallpapers, and maybe a couple of games that worked only on your model phone—that was basically it. 3G was still relatively new in most of the United States, and our phones were really just that, phones.

When Google bought Android, Inc., it was with the intent to make it easy for you to have the Internet at your fingertips at all time. Google being primarily a search engine, the company stood to earn a lot of money making it so you could always search for something you were looking for. Still, there were problems. To be successful, Google couldn't just offer these features on a single device, and it certainly couldn't offer them on a single carrier. Android needed to be available to as many people as possible, and so Google reached out to companies of all types to form the Open Handset Alliance (OHA). The OHA was formed in late 2007 with 34 companies from around the world. These were companies of all types, ranging from carriers like T-Mobile and Sprint, software companies like PacketVideo and eBay, device manufacturers like Motorola and HTC, and chipset manufacturers such as Intel and nVidia. The goal was for each of these companies to come together and collaborate on solutions that everyone in the OHA would directly benefit from.

Huge companies from all over the world putting their combined knowledge and skill into a single project could only result in both direct and indirect benefits across the world. For example, look at most feature phone and smartphones today. You will see that 90 percent of them use the same charging socket to power their devices, and many of those also double as the method to connect the device to your computer. It's only through collaborations on this scale that we could see such a change.

Google wasn't satisfied with a mere 34 companies, either. The Open Handset Alliance grows bigger still even today, with more than 70 companies involved. Collaboration on this scale needed to be more than just companies communicating. The collaboration needed to be unfettered by red tape and proprietary ownership. In the spirit of this collaboration, everything that comes from the Open Handset Alliance is designed to be open source.

WHAT IS OPEN SOURCE?

There are many ways to describe open source. The concept was originally designed so that communities of programmers could collaborate quickly and efficiently. Anything that was generated could simply be shared with anyone involved with the project, and when the project is published for use, the code that was used to create the project becomes publicly available for anyone else to use and help.

Basically, anything that is open source is published so that someone with the skills needed is able to improve on that code, allowing an open source project to continually grow outside of the community that originally created the idea.

THE ANDROID OPEN SOURCE PROJECT

In the true spirit of open source, Google maintains a massive web site specifically for anyone who wants to download and build their own Android; it also offers a submission system for developers. When a developer comes up with a new feature for Android, the developer has the ability to submit their change to Google. This huge collection of change submissions is moderated full-time by Google employees, and features that meet their standards are added into the next version of Android.

This method of growth, combined with Google's own team of programmers, allows for new features to be thought up, written, and implemented in an incredibly short amount of time. As if this download and submission system weren't enough, the Community section of the web site offers a combination of ways to communicate with other developers, be it via forum, Google Group, mailing list, or IRC. This collaborative effort ensures that even half-baked ideas are brought to fruition and guarantees that Android is always on the bleeding edge, ready for that "next big thing." If you are interested in joining the Android developer community, head to http://source.android.com.

ANDY, THE ANDROID "MASCOT"

Since the Android operating system can be manipulated by anyone, it's not always going to look quite the same on every device. One of the quick, whimsical things that was done to fix this was to give Android an icon that would help it stand out. Amid many of the devices now running Android, you will see Andy, the little green robot (as shown in Figure 1–1). It's been given several names, referenced on the Google campus as the "bugdroid" and "Andy." The icon has been used in several places within the operating system, even riding a skateboard in the bootloader.

> **NOTE:** The bootloader is an internal part of the operating system that is responsible for loading Android in the Dalvik Virtual Machine. This is covered in greater detail in Chapter 12.

Figure 1–1. *Android icon: the bugdroid*

Andy has been seen on many devices and has developed a following that rivals the operating system itself. There are countless web sites with memorabilia like stickers and decals with the character, while more in-depth web sites offer everything from T-shirts and plushies of the character. In 2009 a large group of Android fans gathered in Austin, Texas, for an Android-focused get-together, a celebration that is now carried out every year, with an audience in the thousands. While Google does sell its own licensed shirts and accessories with the little green robot on them, the fan-made items from beanies to lanyards and even action figures are in much greater demand.

The T-Mobile G1

In October 2008, five whole years after Android's conception but only a year after the formation of the Open Handset Alliance, the first Android device was born. In a massive collaboration, the T-Mobile G1 (shown in Figure 1–2) was released first in the United States, and then around the world by early 2009. The device was widely seen as Google's response to Apple's iPhone, which was first released in 2007. The G1 offered a physical keyboard that was hidden under the screen until slid out for use. The hinge mechanism that slid the screen away to reveal the keyboard was innovative and was the first of a long list of future devices that began to use similar technology. The G1 was the original Android device and brought with it the desire for companies all around the world to incorporate Android into their device offerings.

Figure 1–2. *The T-Mobile G1*

The Motorola Droid

True to Google's original goal, each of the U.S. carriers and many more around the world soon had plans to offer Android in their line-up. T-Mobile, which already had plans to release four more Android phones in 2009, was ahead of Sprint and AT&T, which had quickly adopted their own strategies for Android deployment. Verizon was the last to the table but had planned a much bigger dive into Android once they decided to join in.

Enter Motorola, a founding member of the Open Handset Alliance, which had already released the Motorola Cliq to T-Mobile. Motorola entered into a partnership with Verizon to help shape Android's explosively popular future. Motorola, which had not had a truly successful phone since the RAZR in 2005, was rapidly approaching bankruptcy and needed a hit. In what seemed like a last-ditch effort to keep the company afloat, Verizon and Motorola released the Motorola Droid in November 2009. The Droid was released exclusively with the latest version of the Android operating system, and its name utilized a trademark by LucasFilm, the owners of the *Star Wars* series.

The Droid was greeted with explosive sales and was one of the driving forces behind the more than 900 percent growth Android saw in 2009 over 2008. Today, Motorola remains the manufacturer of one of the most popular line of Android devices, going so far as to release multiple sequels to the Droid line. Today, the Droid line is home to seven different phones, all exclusive to Verizon.

The Google Nexus One

To encourage the development of apps in Android, Google has taken several steps along the way to encourage developers to make bigger, better, and more feature-rich apps. Arguably the most significant step taken by Google was the release of the Nexus One (shown in Figure 1–3) and the start of its Nexus line of devices. The original intent of the Nexus One was twofold. Google wanted to offer a device that was free from the carrier. It wanted a device you could purchase from Google and add to your network of choice, without being stuck in a contract or having to follow the carrier's terms of service regarding device policies. The device was also very easy for developers to test applications on, offering a powerful device to ensure that it would run on all Android phones. Additionally, when an update was available to the Android operating system, it would be released to the Nexus line first to ensure developers had time to make any adjustments or to add new features to their apps.

 VS

Figure 1–3. *The Nexus One and Nexus S*

> **NOTE:** The Nexus line of phones all run Android as though it was compiled via the Android Open Source Project. It's commonly known as "Stock Android" or "the Google Experience." The second part of this chapter will cover more on the "flavors of Android."

To date, there has not yet been a "Nexus" tablet. Google has collaborated with many different companies to bring its devices to the market but nothing with the Nexus branding like its phones. If Google does ever decide to release a Nexus tablet, it will be like its phones in that it will come to market with the latest version of Android, available only to that device before updates are released to the other tablets.

The iPad

By 2010, it was clear that the cell phone market was dominated by the choice between the iPhone on AT&T or any of the now dozens of Android-powered devices in all shapes and sizes across every U.S. network and dozens of other networks around the world. The availability and options alone made it easy to see why Android was so quickly gaining on the bar Apple had set. The battle for market share was getting closer and closer, when in early 2010 Apple changed things up a bit and moved the iPhone onto the big screen.

The iPad (shown in Figure 1–4) has been hailed as a revolutionary device, accomplishing what no one before had been able to do. It combined the functionality of its already immensely popular smartphone onto a 10-inch screen, giving its audience the ability to not only enjoy their favorite apps but also be extremely productive. The concept of a tablet was not new. Tablet computers had been tried several times in the past, running Windows, Linux, or even much earlier the Apple Newton tablet. The problem in the past was that the software really did not support the design. There was no touch-specific design to the desktop operating systems we had all been used to using. So, now the Apple tablet was born; it would only make sense for Android to respond in the same fashion as it had in the smartphone world.

Figure 1–4. *The Apple iPad*

Android tablets offer the same functionality that an Android phone offers, just like an iPad's relationship to an iPhone. The critical difference between the two tablets' operating systems is the way apps interact between devices. With every Android device, logging into the Play Store with your account grants you access to any app you have paid for. When you install that app, it will function the same way on your tablet as it did on your phone. This is not the case on the iPad. You must purchase an "iPad-specific" app that supports the larger screen. If you install an app that was meant for an iPhone, it will only take up as much space on your screen as it would on an iPhone.

Which Android Tablet Is for Me?

Just like Android phones, Android tablets come in all shapes and sizes, designed for all kinds of different kinds of users. What's important when considering your Android tablet is to first understand what you want to do with it. Are you interested in doing a lot of reading? Will you be typing a lot, say for schoolwork or at the office? Are you the kind of person who plays a lot of video games? Will your tablet live in your living room and control your home theater? Would you take your tablet with you everywhere you go? Your tablet should be customized for your life and your needs, you shouldn't have to teach yourself how to be comfortable with something else.

Screen Type

Arguably the most important part of your Android tablet is the screen. It doesn't really matter what kind of processor you have or how much memory it has if you are not comfortable using your screen. If you can't read the text, if you can't easily control your apps because the screen isn't what you need, what good is it? It's all about how you use the device.

- *Capacitive touchscreen*: This is currently the most common kind of screen found in devices like smartphones and tablets. These screens require the touch of a finger in order to control the device and are made of either glass or special plastics. A capacitive screen will increase the price of a device.

- *Resistive touchscreen*: These types of screens are commonly found on "budget tablets" or screens used in fast-food restaurants. They are much cheaper to make than capacitive screens and are much less accurate. Screens like this will not be good to play games on but are great if you have fingernails or if you wear gloves a lot because they do not require the touch of a finger. Devices like these are commonly sold with a small plastic stylus to make them easier to use.

- *OLED display*: This type of display will show you rich, vibrant colors that are perfect for games, movies, and pictures. Because of the construction of the display, however, things like text do not display as well as other screen types, making it harder to use as an e-book.

- *LCD display*: This is the same kind of display that is most commonly seen in computer monitors. These colors on this screen are not a good as an AMOLED screen, but text looks better. These screens are great all-around screens.

- *Pixel Qi Display*: This is a relatively new kind of screen; these displays are capable of both brilliant and rich colors as well as transfer to an E-Ink display. This technology allows for the best kind of display for enjoying media as well as operating as a low-power, Kindle-like display for viewing text. These displays are generally more expensive but offer the best experience to date.

Each of these technologies fits a use case. The most common combination of technologies you will see is a capacitive touchscreen on an OLED display. These are typical of higher-end devices, like the Samsung Galaxy Tab.

Screen Size

There stands a pretty good chance that your hand is not the same size as everyone else. Because of this harsh reality, you may not be comfortable with the same size device as everyone else. Fortunately, Android allows manufacturers to release devices of all sizes for us to use. There are currently four typical sizes for an Android tablet.

- *Less than 7-inch*: These devices bridge the gap between smartphone and computer, since the largest smartphone/tablet hybrids to date are the Samsung Galaxy Note and the 5-inch Dell Streak. These devices are just about as pocketable as a cell phone. If GPS is included these devices, they make great in-vehicle devices that can provide entertainment and navigation.

- *7-inch tablets*: This form factor is ideal for users interested in an e-book reader, web browser, or media player that is extremely portable. Seven-inch devices fit great in a back pocket, a purse, or a suit coat pocket. These devices can often come ready to work in a business environment with a physical keyboard that can be attached or with a suction cup mount to enjoy media or navigation in your car. Some also come equipped with the ability to add more memory or to connect to your television to enjoy your media in a home theater.

- *8- to 10-inch tablets:* These larger devices are typically used for enjoying media, browsing, and playing games on a larger screen. They are much less portable but typically come with features that more nearly match those of a traditional laptop, such as USB ports, dedicated video output slots and so on. The cost for these devices is typically the highest of the group because of the added cost involved in their creation.

> **NOTE:** There are currently no tablets on the market that are larger than 10 inches, but the sky is the limit, so it is assumed it is only a matter of time before larger devices are seen.

Internet Access

One of the really great things that any tablet will be able to do in some form or another is connect to the Internet. Google is first and foremost a web search company, so it makes good sense that Android would be driven by the Web. It's not a requirement that you be connected to the Internet, but when you are, you have a much more powerful device in your hands. By connecting your tablet to the Internet, you unite Android with all of Google's Internet-based services immediately, and your tablet becomes in sync with what Google calls the *cloud*.

Google's cloud is a massive collection of very powerful computers all around the world. The job of these computers is to store all of the information you give to your Android tablet. Maybe it's a list of contacts, pictures, documents, e-mail, and more. Google saves all of this information on both your tablet and in the cloud. This gives you the unique opportunity to always have access to this information. Maybe you left the tablet at home but need to get your friend's cell phone number? Log in to your Gmail account from any computer, and all of your contacts are there. Google's Picasa service stores your photos online and allows you to access them from anywhere. Play Books allows you to read any of millions of books, and it saves what page you are on. Now, let's say something really bad happens and your tablet is destroyed, right in the middle of a book. If you head to your computer, to your phone, or even to another tablet and log in, Google will bring your online experience back to you just the way you left it.

Wi-Fi or 3G/4G?

As we have seen, being connected to the Internet can be a huge help, but it's important to decide whether it is worth it to you to be connected to the Internet at all time. There are many places all around us, especially in larger cities, that allow you to connect to public wireless Internet for free, and it is probably a pretty good bet that you even have wireless Internet in your home. Connecting your tablet to the Internet this way does not cost you anything extra because it uses your existing Internet that you already pay a provider for. Additionally, many Android phones are capable of generating a wireless network or mobile hotspot, giving you the ability to share your mobile Internet with your tablet.

Creating a mobile hotspot with your phone is harsh on your battery life. Unless you have the ability to plug your phone in somewhere for power, it's unlikely your phone will last all day doing this. The same Internet service you would receive from your cell phone can be put on your tablet, however, giving you Internet everywhere you are. This service is not free and typically means you need to pay for a separate line of service on your cellular plan. If you purchased your tablet from a cell phone carrier, you likely will need to add a new data plan to your account.

The choice that you make here is really one of convenience vs. price. If you do not feel the need to pay that additional monthly rate for Internet on your tablet or if you are just simply near Wi-Fi networks enough that you would never use the feature, you should make sure your tablet is "Wi-Fi only" upon purchase. This typically decreases the cost of the tablet because it will not come with the ability to use mobile networks.

What You Need to Know About 4G

If you have chosen to get yourself a tablet that connects to a mobile network for Internet, you have likely heard a thing or two about this thing called 4G. It is important that you understand exactly what this means, the costs associated with this faster technology, and whether you are getting the best 4G service.

Before you make any purchases, you need to reach out to the carrier you will be purchasing the service from and ensure that 4G service will be available in the areas you frequently travel, as well as where you live. Once you have found whether 4G service is available in your area, it is important to then see which "4G" service is being offered by your carrier of choice. There are several options depending on your area.

- *LTE*: This is an acronym for Long Term Evolution; the technology was built as the next step away from the existing 3G networks used across the world today. This network is capable of great speed at low latency, making it comparable to the performance of many home Internet services. LTE networks are able to be continually upgraded to be much faster than they are today.

- *HSPA+*: This technology is an upgrade of the existing HSPA service offered by many GSM carriers around the world. This technology is an improvement in that it offers an increase in speed, but the technology suffers from the same latency issues as HSPA, and its performance decreases rapidly as you leave the radius of a broadcast point.

- *WiMax*: One of the first 4G networks, WiMax is deployed in the United States only by Sprint. WiMax is considered in many places to be just as fast as HSPA+ and benefits from being available in most major cities in the United States.

Each implementation of 4G is just a little bit different, but if your tablet supports one of these wireless technologies, you will be able to access the Internet at greater speeds, allowing you to take greater advantage of features such as video chat, video editing, streaming media, and anything else you might find.

Understanding Android User Interface Options

Andy Rubin, the CEO of Android, Inc., and now the VP of engineering and head of the Android project at Google, was recently quoted about how Android is viewed by Google.

"We consider ourselves the shepherd of Android. With Open Source, you don't really know what's going to happen. Innovation doesn't just happen in this building, it happens all around us."

Android is open source, so anyone can grab a copy and add features they deem necessary. It's not a requirement that changes be submitted to Google through the

Android Open Source Project. In fact, there are several major versions of Android on phones, and soon tablets, today. These versions are made by different manufacturers in an attempt to improve the Android user experience or to add features that the manufacturers offered on previous smartphones. This causes a slightly different user experience depending on who the manufacturer of your device is, allowing you to choose based on what features interest you.

Manufacturers are not the only ones with an idea of "what's best" for their users. Some carriers in the United States have developed software that is available only for devices sold on their networks. Sprint and Verizon are the most noted in these developments. The SprintID service allows a user to quickly theme their device with any of hundreds of options, and any apps that would function with that theme are preinstalled. The NFL app on Sprint is also an exclusive that gives users all the latest football statistics and videos straight from the NFL, but it is exclusive to Sprint. Verizon's VCast service, an on-demand media service that was originally designed for feature phones, is now available exclusively to Verizon Wireless customers.

These "exclusive" items between carrier and manufacturer are not without equal. Like many things in the Android ecosystem, an app in the Play Store has been developed to match the features offered by that service. It has often been said that no two Android devices look quite the same as a result of all of the ways you can customize your device, and we will show you how. For now, however, we can go over some of the bigger "flavors" of Android.

HTC Sense

Sense is the result of years of software evolution at HTC. The company has spent a lot of time focused on the user experience, despite the operating system beneath. When given such an open platform as Android to mold, the software team at HTC set out to create a user experience that focuses on a highly stylized user interface with large, whole-page widgets to access features. It's not just Android that has been modified, either. To offer a complete solution, HTC has reached into nearly every core app and modified it to enhance the experience for the user (see Figure 1–5).

Figure 1–5. *The HTC Flyer Android tablet*

- *Desk clock*: Arguably the distinguishing feature in Sense is a large clock widget that typically occupies the top half of your main page on the home screen. Aside from offering the time in very large font, the widget also animates the current weather in your area on the screen. When you unlock your phone, the weather will animate off the widget and onto the whole phone. If it's raining, raindrops will fall onto your screen; when it's sunny, the rays of sunlight will beam from the center of the widget. These animations typically last only a moment and can be interrupted at any point by touching the screen.

- *People widget*: This is a full-page widget that shows you your contacts and their images if you have associated one with their contact information. The widget will pull any information you have associated with their contact form, including their most recent updates to services like Twitter or Facebook.

- *Friendstream*: As both an app and a widget, Friendstream ties together all of your social networking services such as Twitter, Facebook, MySpace, and so on, and organizes them into a single app to scroll through, instead of needing to access these separately. Should you want to post something to any of these service, you can do this within the app.

- *Music*: Sense's Music app looks very different from "stock" Android, offering users the ability to visually navigate their albums instead of just scrolling down a playlist. Additionally, the ability to pause a song or skip tracks is embedded in the lock screen to HTC Sense, allowing you to control your music without unlocking your phone and navigating to the Music app.

- *Camera*: The Camera app has been themed with menu icons that make it easier to quickly adjust camera settings, switch from camera to camcorder, and flip to the front-facing camera. Additional features, such as automatically rotating the picture type from portrait to landscape when the phone is turned and camera effects such as sepia and black and white, have been added to the Camera app as well.

The highly stylized nature of HTC Sense comes at a price. The constantly evolving nature of Android is such that feature updates are released on a six-month cycle, including the latest from the Android Open Source Project. An HTC Sense device will not receive these updates until they have been stylized and modified by HTC, causing Sense devices to lag behind by as much as three months in some cases. Once an update is available, HTC released an OTA update to its devices to implement the new features.

Samsung TouchWiz

Samsung has also heavily modified its releases of Android devices in order to offer a solution it thinks is better for the user. Like SenseUI, TouchWiz was used by Samsung before Android and is still used on its BADA platform in some parts of the world. TouchWiz (shown in Figure 1–6) incorporates popular visual elements from many popular user interfaces.

Figure 1–6. *Touchwiz for tablets made by Samsung*

■ *Numbered pages*: Unlike the traditional or "stock" home screen where the center page is the landing page when the home button is pressed, TouchWiz includes a modified page system that allows for any of the pages to be selected as the primary. Additionally, it is made easy to rapidly jump in between pages by tapping the numbered dots at the top of the home screen.

■ *Customized launcher*: Traditionally, the launcher organizes your apps alphabetically and enables you to scroll vertically along the list of apps. Touchwiz aligns the apps horizontally so you can drag your finger from side to side to view your apps. Additionally, the apps can be placed in whichever order you want in the launcher rather than alphabetically. App icons are displayed with a colorful background allowing them to exist in a uniform shape and size.

> **NOTE:** The icons on either side of the launcher in TouchWiz are replaceable. By long-pressing on the icons to the left or right of the launcher, you effectively free the app to be placed on the home screen or in the trashcan to be sent back to the app drawer. You are able to place any app on either side of the launcher.

- *Custom widgets*: Included in all TouchWiz devices are the Social widget, which combines your Twitter, Myspace, Facebook, and so on, into a single scrollable feed on your home screen, and a daily report widget. This widget pulls information from news sources, weather, stocks, and more, into a widget for you to access.

Like with SenseUI, TouchWiz must be fully adapted in order to update to the next version of Android, putting it out of sync with Google's update cycle. When changes are released, Samsung engineers must implement the TouchWiz features and thoroughly test them before releasing an update. To date, Samsung is the only company that has not released device updates OTA and instead has had consumers install it manually via their computers. This process requires a Windows PC to complete.

Amazon Kindle Fire

Many users of the original Amazon Kindle have wanted their amazing e-book readers to do a little bit more. In November 2011, Amazon released the Kindle Fire, a 7-inch tablet based on Android (see Figure 1–7).

Amazon heavily modified the version of Android used on the Fire, so much that it does not have any of the features that Google includes with any other version of Android. Amazon has replaced those features with its own versions. Unlike most Android tablets, Amazon will not be pressed to release the most recent version of Android, and many of the features that exist with Android tablets will be added only if Amazon chooses to do so.

- *Amazon App Store*: Replacing the Play Store for Android devices is an app store maintained and controlled by Amazon. Among the significant features that separate the Amazon App Store from the Play Store is a free app of the day.

- *Amazon Movies and Music*: All of the TV shows, music, and movies available for rental or purchase on Amazon.com are available on the Kindle Fire. Amazon.com users who have an Amazon Prime account can access free streaming content from the Kindle Fire.

- *Amazon Silk Browser*: Replacing the stock Android browser, Amazon's Silk browser is customized for the Kindle Fire, allowing users to access complex web sites much faster than the stock Android mobile browser.

Figure 1–7. *The Amazon Kindle Fire*

Stock Android 3.0 (Honeycomb)

Android 3.0 is the first version of Android designed specifically for devices that exceed the typical sizes of smartphones. Dubbed Honeycomb as part of Google's alphabetical version naming system, Android 3.0 is the basis for most Android tablets on the market and will be the platform on which most of this book will focus. It is Google's intention to both provide an enhanced experience for tablets and not drift so far away from the smartphone-optimized design that there is a tremendous learning curve.

There are some significant differences, however, that create a very different user experience (see Figure 1–8).

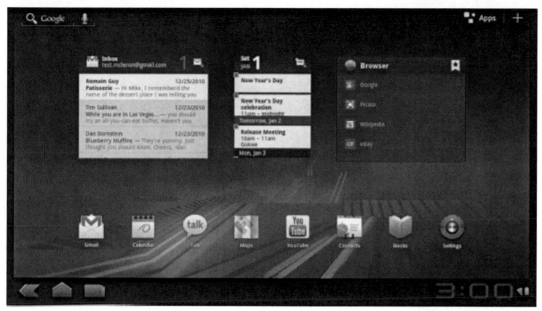

Figure 1–8. *Android 3.0 "Honeycomb"*

- *More space on the home screen*: The 3.0 design makes each page on your home screen capable of holding much, much more than on your phone. On your 4-inch screen, it makes sense to have a widget take up an entire page, but that design isn't really that useful on a 7-inch or 10-inch screen. Now, if you could fill a page with three or four of those full-screen widgets side by side, it would offer you much greater productivity gains.

- *Dedicated multitasking button*: Android 3.0 was designed to not require physical buttons for "back" or "home" and replaces them with buttons on the screen. Because of this change, you can no longer long-press on the home button to gain access to your recently opened apps. Now that ability has been given its own button, located next to the home and back buttons for quick access.

- *Optimized GApps*: Included in the Android 3.0 SDK are the tools necessary to optimize your app for larger screens. To offer you examples and to optimize their own apps, Google has modified its Gmail and Google Calendar apps to take advantage of the increase in real estate by offering a version of Gmail that looks much more like a traditional mail client found on a computer (see Figure 1–9).

Figure 1–9. *The Motorola Xoom running Android 3.0*

- *Google Maps revisited*: To allow Google Maps to load faster in any environment and to provide added functionality to the navigation experience, Google Maps has been given a bit of a facelift. Zooming down to ground level in Google Maps will now reveal a 3D navigation experience, shown as the buildings rise up to meet you when you have zoomed down far enough. The 3D rendering of cities allows for faster recognition and navigation without requiring a very fast Internet connection or using too much processing power.

- *New Camera interface*: Proving that there is so much that can be done with so much screen, the Camera app for Android has been adjusted so you can quickly make settings changes to get that picture taken. To the right of the screen is a series of rings with menu option inside, allowing you to hold the device still and make changes on the fly.

- *Desktop-quality browser*: Google makes its own browser called Chrome. The browser inside Android is not called Chrome, but it sure looks like it now. The ability to quickly add and manipulate "tabs" in the browser has been added so you can have multiple topics open on your browser and be able to quickly switch between them.

Additionally, an "Incognito" mode, similar to the one found in Chrome has been added, allowing you to browse without saving passwords or leaving behind any trace of your browsing history. This gives you the ability to hand the tablet to a friend and not be concerned that you accidentally saved his password.

▪ *Google Movie Studio*: A new addition to the suite of apps offered by Google, Movie Studio allows you to take pictures or video shot with a tablet, phone, or camera and edit them into a video right on the tablet. Movie Studio offers features such as text insertion, music tracks, and interactive pan and zoom and fade features, to name a few. Google Movie Studio takes full advantage of the power and mobility of a tablet-sized screen and allows you to publish these movies instantly to YouTube.

▪ *Support for more powerful processors*: The mobile world has seen some truly impressive growth over the last few years. While mobile computing is not as powerful as what you would see in a traditional desktop or laptop, that gap is closing quickly. If the phone in your hand is nothing more than a tiny computer, it stands to reason that someone is going to want their tablet to be just a bit more powerful, and Google has accounted for this. Dual-core processors, similar in design to what you see in a traditional computer, only smaller, offer the power necessary to do things like watch a movie and chat online while uploading a photo library to Facebook.

Android 4.0 "Ice Cream Sandwich"

Google took all of the features and functionality of Android 3.0 and issued thousands of very small changes to create a polished new operating system. Android 4.0, shown in Figure 1–10, has been visually redesigned from the ground up to offer a more elegant look and feel. On top of the visual enhancements, Android 4.0 offers huge performance increases in both speed and battery life.

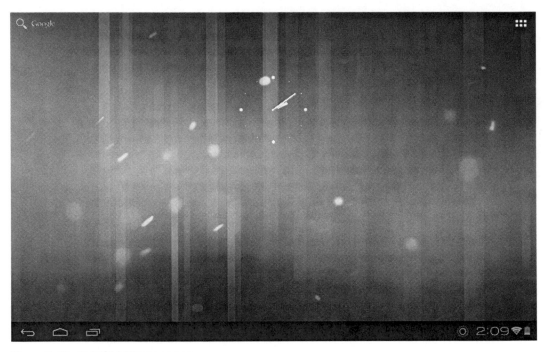

Figure 1–10. *Android 4.0 home screen*

FRAGMENTATION: DISPELLING THE MYTH

By now, you have probably realized that not all Android tablets are created equal. Different sizes, different ways to access the Internet, and different versions of Android separate the choices you would see when walking into an electronics store or shopping online. This chapter has covered many possibilities in the Android ecosystem for you to choose from. In fact, with so many choices available, critics of Android's ability to function across a multitude of options have given it the nickname *fragmentation* since the user experience is not the same on each and every device. On the surface, this issue could be seen as a very real problem. After all, if you have to relearn how to use their phone or tablet each time you pick up a new device, it's not helpful, right?

As it turns out, Google has taken many steps to ensure that the core of Android is functional on every device it includes GApps with. Included in the Android SDK, with the support of the Android Developer Community and the Android Open Source Project, are the tools needed to make sure that as a developer your app will work the same across all Android devices. On top of that, all members of the Open Handset Alliance have agreed to maintain and update their devices as updates become available to ensure that no device, and no user, is left behind.

The Android "Budget Tablet" Without Google

Many manufacturers, eager to get Android onto their tablets and into the hands of users, opted to release devices before getting approval from Google to use GApps on their devices. Some manufacturers attempt to create their own app store to install apps. Some manufacturers released tablets with no app store, making it so apps had to be downloaded from the Internet and installed manually. Some manufacturers opted to put the Play Store on their tablet without Google's permission, forcing legal action upon themselves as a result. All of these tablets are not approved by Google to have the Play Store on them for various reasons. These "budget tablets" are almost all Wi-Fi only devices, many with resistive touchscreens on varying sizes, allowing them to be comparably inexpensive.

Android is free for anyone to make and use, but the Play Store is not open source; it is owned by Google. The Play Store is connected to a user's Google Wallet account, a Google service that can store credit cards, addresses, purchasing history, and more. Because such sensitive information is within the Play Store, Google requires that every version of Android that has the Play Store be approved by Google. If the version of Android meets its criteria, the Play Store is clear to be installed.

Summary

There are plenty of things to keep in mind when deciding which tablet is for you. Beyond simply understanding the capabilities and limits of these devices, it's important to consider exactly what kind of user you are and what type of device would be best suited for your needs. By addressing your personal needs, you will be able to quickly decide on the tablet that's right for you and the accessories that are best suited for your use.

Chapter 2

Choosing the Right Tablet

One of the many advantages of the Android operating system is its ability to run on a variety of devices. Since each person's needs are different, it is unlikely one tablet will serve every person's needs. Everyone should have a device that fits their specific uses. In this chapter, we will cover the various features and services found on typical Android devices, how they might apply to your needs, and how to choose the best of tablet for you.

Features

Which features should you consider? Since different companies make Android tablets, some Android tablets will be very different from others. These differences may be important to you depending on how you choose to use your tablet. The following are the four most important features to consider when choosing your device.

Size

When it comes to purchasing an Android tablet, the size of the screen can be an important factor. After all, a tablet really is little more than just a screen that you interact with, so you should choose a size that's most comfortable for you. You should make this decision based on how you feel when you use the device. Entertainment, enterprise, student, and travel users all have different needs that could be met by the appropriate screen size.

- Tablets with screens that are less than 7 inches are extremely portable but not very good for typing more than a few sentences at a time.

- Tablets with 10-inch screens are great for productivity, but the added size and weight often make them just about as portable as a laptop. Additionally, they typically require some kind of stand or dock to be used for any significant length of time.

- Seven-inch tablets offer a comfortable blend of portability and productivity without really optimizing for either. The size lends itself to being useful in most circumstances because the tablet is small enough to be operated with one hand.

Cameras

Like many cell phones, most tablets can be used to take pictures. The cameras on tablets vary in quality and functionality. If having a camera on your tablet is important to you, you should be aware of your options.

- **Front-facing camera**: Typically these cameras are small, with a resolution of less than 3 megapixels, but they will usually let you engage in a video chat.

- **Rear-facing camera**: These cameras range in quality and will typically produce images and video of the same quality as the rear-facing camera on your cell phone. These cameras are almost always capable of taking better pictures and recording video than a front-facing camera.

- **Rotating camera**: These cameras typically have the same qualities rear-facing cameras have but are engineered to rotate from the front to the back of the tablet. This style is less common.

Memory

The ability to store documents, pictures, music, movies, or anything else is extremely important on a tablet. Just like with the computer, however, the amount of storage at your disposal directly affects the price of your tablet. The following are the types of storage available.

- **Onboard memory**: This memory comes built into the tablet and cannot be removed or upgraded. The storage capacities of these devices range from 8GB to 64GB, and the cost goes up exponentially the more storage you have. What you see is what you get, but this type of memory is generally faster than removable storage. The downside to this storage type is that should anything happen to the memory on your tablet (a power surge while connected to power, a violent drop to a hard surface, and so on), the device will be rendered useless, and you will need to replace the entire device.

- **Removable storage**: Some tablets provide the ability to expand your onboard storage through an expandable memory slot. The memory slot typically supports a micro SD card, which can be purchased in a wide variety of sizes based on your need. Currently, micro SD cards can be purchased in measurements of both size and speed (*class*), and increasing either will directly affect the price. Currently, micro SD cards do not come in capacities higher than 32GB, and the price for those cards is significant and usually not included in the price of your tablet.

Internet

No matter what kind of user you are, you're bound to use your tablet to access the Internet. What is important, however, is that you identify whether you *always* need the Internet and are willing to pay for that privilege. Here are the options you're going to encounter:

- **Wi-Fi only**: You probably have wireless Internet at home, at work, or at school, so you may not need to be connected to the Internet everywhere you go.

- **Mobile Internet 3G/4G contract**: As we discussed in Chapter 1, you can purchase an always-on service from your carrier for a monthly fee. Prices vary from carrier to carrier, and you are typically required to enter into a one- or two-year contract.

  - **Mobile hotspot**: Typically offered for an additional fee on top of your contract price, this gives you the ability to share your 3G/4G service with any Wi-Fi enabled device.

  - **Tethering**: Similar to mobile hotspot, this gives you the ability to share your 3G/4G service with a computer by connecting a USB cable from your tablet to the computer.

- **Pay-as-you-go mobile Internet 3G/4G**: Some carriers have plans that allow you to purchase either blocks of data or a single month of service time. To take advantage of this, your tablet must have the 3G/4G equipment inside.

What Kind of User Are You?

Users can generally be classified into groups based on the activities they are most likely to do on their tablets. Identifying your needs based on these groups of activities can help you choose a tablet with the combination of features that works best for you. For example, which of the following profiles would you say best fits your lifestyle?

A Road Warrior

Your tablet doubles as your GPS. It sticks with you at all times and needs to be incredibly portable. The Internet is always at your fingertips. Your laptop or desktop computer does all the heavy lifting when you need it.

- Mobile Internet
- Seven-inch screen or smaller
- Front-facing/rear-facing cameras
- Removable storage
- Mobile hotspot

A Tech Gearhead

You need the best of everything. You need the biggest screen, the fastest processor, and the most storage. You have the best gadget there is right now, and you'll have the one that comes out next week too.

- Ten-inch screen
- Mobile Internet
- Removable storage
- Rotating camera

A Student or Teacher

You need a "New Age" typewriter, access to all of your Internet resources, and every one of your books wrapped up in a box no bigger than a stack of papers. What matters to you the most is the ability to type comfortably and the ability to read no matter where you are.

- Any kind of Internet connection
- Seven to 10-inch screen
- Onboard storage
- Pay-as-you-go Internet

A Music and Movie Junkie

For you, you need a high-quality screen, good stereo speakers, and a battery strong enough to get you through a couple of movies, your favorite TV shows, or maybe just playing music at your desk all day. Lots of storage and a fast Internet connection are two of your best friends.

- Removable storage
- Seven to 10-inch screen
- Mobile Internet
- Cameras optional

A Bookworm

A big screen isn't nearly as important as the ability to take your books, magazines, newspapers, and PDFs everywhere you go. Even though it holds thousands of books inside, it still shouldn't weigh more than your favorite novel.

- Wi-Fi only

- Seven-inch screen

- Cameras optional

- Onboard storage

A Mobile Office User

Since most of your time is spent in a car, on a plane, or in anyone's office but yours, it's important that you be able to work from anywhere. A constant Internet connection, a big keyboard, and the ability to jump into a videoconference with the boss at any time are the features you need.

- Ten-inch screen

- Mobile Internet

- Front-facing camera

- Removable storage

- Mobile hotspot

Where Should You Buy Your Tablet?

We've narrowed things down a bit to help you pick a tablet that will best fit your needs. You've probably seen some commercials, maybe have read some reviews, and may have even gone into a couple stores to get your hands on one or two. Now it's time to go out and get yours! Where's the best place to do this? Here are some options:

- **Carrier stores**: This is the best place to go if you're looking for a tablet with a 3G/4G contract. Carriers will also stock all the official accessories for your new tablet.

- **Electronics stores**: Many of these stores will offer a wide selection of both Wi-Fi only and 3G/4G contract tablets across a variety of carriers. Additionally, the stores will carry both the official accessories as well as less expensive accessories made by third-party manufacturers.

- **Warehouse stores**: High-volume warehouse style stores will likely be the least expensive place to get your tablet, but their selection is usually limited to Wi-Fi only models. This type of store isn't likely to carry many accessories for your device.

Warranty or Insurance?

When purchasing your tablet, you will likely be asked whether you are interested in either an extended warranty or an insurance policy on your device. Although these are an additional expense, typically they give you the ability to inexpensively replace your device should almost anything happen to it. So, what's the difference between the two?

- **Insurance**: Typically offered by carriers, an insurance policy charges a small fee each month you own the device. Should anything happen to tablet that is covered by insurance, you would be given a new tablet.

- **Warranty**: Most commonly seen in electronics stores, the warrantee service is an additional fee usually based on a percentage of the cost of the device you pay up front with no monthly fee. The warranty covers your device for a fixed amount of time and offers replacement of the device should anything happen that is covered by the warranty.

Accessories?

Regardless of which tablet you choose, there may be a few things that you would like to go with your device to make it more useful. Depending on where you buy your tablet, you may be able pick up accessories specifically designed for your device. The following are among the most popular:

- **Case**: Just about half of the surface area of every tablet is glass, and any scratches in the surface of the glass can seriously affect the way the screen responds to touch. A case that covers the screen when not in use is generally a good idea. With some models, the part of the case that covers the screen will also double as a stand when folded back, making it easier for you to type on the virtual device keyboard.

- **Dock**: This accessory allows you to charge your device in an upright position, allowing you to work while it charges without messing with wires, as shown in Figure 2–1. Most docks provide additional features, such as a speaker for music or a magnetic charging connection so that you can quickly remove the device.

- **Keyboard**: Typing on a virtual keyboard is not easy for everyone, and most people type faster on a physical keyboard. Most tablet keyboards connect via Bluetooth and include a stand to hold the tablet while you type. Figure 2–1 shows a tablet dock and keyboard.

Figure 2–1. *Tablet dock and keyboard*

Unboxing Your Tablet

Hooray, you've picked a tablet! Now the fun parts can happen. Before you get home and tear everything out of the box, leaving your bedroom/office/kitchen a glorious mess of shredded paper and plastic, there are a few things you should do.

- **Make sure your box doesn't do tricks**: Strange as this sounds, it's not terribly uncommon. Some manufacturers offer clever things you can do with the packaging as freebies. For example, the packaging for the Barnes and Noble Nook Color folds back on itself and sticks together magnetically to form an inexpensive cardboard stand for your tablet. Before you destroy the box, make sure it doesn't do something cool.

- **Manufacturer's warranty information**: Regardless of whether you purchased additional warranty services from the store where you bought your tablet, most manufacturers offer a one-year limited warranty, and the documentation for that is in your box for you to fill out and send in.

Most tablets come with both a power cord to charge your device and a USB cable to connect your tablet to a computer. Depending on the power requirements of your tablet, your tablet manufacturer will likely choose one of the following cable configurations:

- **A single removable cable**: Such a cable will have a USB port on one end and a special connector on the other that is unique to your device, such as the one shown in Figure 2–2. To charge your tablet at a wall outlet, the manufacturer may include a small power adapter that can accept the USB connector.

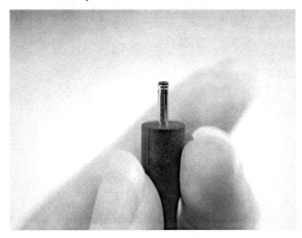

Figure 2–2. *Tablet power cord*

- **Separate power cord and USB cable**: Your manufacturer may decide to include a separate cord to charge your tablet and one to connect your tablet to the computer. This way, you can charge and sync your tablet simultaneously.

- **PC dock**: If you choose to purchase a dock, you'll likely be able to connect your tablet to your desk or laptop computer and charge it simultaneously simply by setting your tablet in the dock.

Now that you've unpacked your Android tablet, let's fire it up!

Setting Up Your Tablet

Your new Android tablet has a lot of individual parts that come together to create a single great device. We're going to take a look at some of the things that are likely to be somewhere on your tablet, as well as some best practices for initial use.

First Charge

Like most electronics, your tablet will come with the battery about a quarter used. Many tablets do not offer the ability to remove the battery, so it is important that you take proper care of this one. On average, the battery is one of the most expensive parts of your device and is not covered by most warranty or insurance policies. Before you take your tablet out to play, there are several things you can do to ensure long battery life.

- **Give it a full charge**: I know it's tempting to turn that new toy on and play until you fall down, but plug it into the wall and allow it to charge for roughly 12 hours before turning it on. This will ensure you have a completely full battery prior to your first use, as indicated by Figure 2–3.

Figure 2–3. *Honeycomb device fully charged*

- **Drain your battery on first use**: During your first use, do not reconnect the tablet to the charger until it is completely drained. Completely empty the battery the first time you use the device, and then fully charge the device again before turning it back on.

Additional Ports

So far we've discussed the various ports that are common on your tablet: the power port, data port (or a port that does both), and the headphone jack. For some of you, there may be a few other slots hanging around, such as the ones shown in Figure 2–4. They will be identified in your user manual; you may find yourself with the following:

- **HDMI port**: Not unlike the USB port in size but shaped slightly differently, the HDMI port is there to allow you to connect your tablet to a television so you can share music, movies, games, or anything else with the bigger screen using a normal HDMI cable. Typically, this will also allow you to view things on your tablet in high(er) definition.

- **Mini HDMI port**: This port will operate in the same way as the full-sized HDMI port but will require a special cable since the port on your tablet is much smaller. These cables can almost always be found where you purchased the tablet.

- **Magnetic strips**: These will be used only for docking your device. Make sure you dock your device *only* to a dock that supports your tablet to avoid any unnecessary hardware issues.

Figure 2–4. *Motorola Xoom ports*

SIM Card

If you have purchased a tablet that supports mobile Internet, you may have a slot for a SIM card. SIM cards, like the one shown in Figure 2–5, are used by GSM carriers (T-Mobile, AT&T) as well as 4G LTE mobile Internet providers (Verizon Wireless, MetroPCS, AT&T). These cards provide your device with the instructions necessary to access the service from your provider. If you purchased your tablet from one of these providers, the card was likely inserted for you at the time of activation. A SIM card is fragile and should be removed from the device only by a professional or with the assistance of a professional. Damage to this card can cause intermittent or low-quality service to the tablet. If you feel there is a problem with your SIM card, contact your provider immediately.

Figure 2-5. *SIM card*

The SIM card stores information in a way that makes it possible to move quickly from one device to another with no interruption in your service. Simply have the SIM card placed in the new device before turning it on, and your mobile Internet service will be there. The mobile Internet service will only ever be provided to the device that the SIM card is currently installed it. But moving the card frequently from one device to another is not recommended as doing so could damage it.

Powering Up

Each manufacturer puts the power button for its models in a slightly different location. Consult your user manual if you can't find it. Press and hold the power button until you see an image on the screen. The device is now on! Give it a couple of seconds to boot up and show you an animation, and you will be ready to use your device for the first time. That power button isn't just for turning the device on or off either. It is also functions as the device's sleep and wake button, so you will be using it often.

Summary

Purchasing a tablet should get the same personal attention as when purchasing a personal computer. Your tablet should be suited to your needs and your preferences and should be available to you at a price that also fits your budget. For many, a tablet bridges the gap between a smartphone and a computer, so it's important that the hardware you choose is something you will be want to use on a regular basis. Now that you have selected a tablet best suited for you, it's time to get it set up and ready to use.

Chapter 3

Creating Your Google Account

One of the greatest features of any Android device is the way it tightly integrates other web-based Google products and services—everything from Gmail to Google Maps—with its own capabilities. So, you'll need a Google account to access these features. (You don't need a Google account to use your tablet, but you won't be able to access the Play Store and other online services without one.) In this chapter, you will learn how to set up your Google account either from your Android tablet or by going directly to Google.com. Of course, if you already have a Google account, you can skip this step entirely, as discussed in the sidebar "Do You Already Have a Google Account?"

In this chapter, we will also cover logging into your Google account on the tablet for the first time and syncing your Google account with your Android tablet.

DO YOU ALREADY HAVE A GOOGLE ACCOUNT?

Chances are that if you currently use any of Google's services or already own an Android phone, then you probably have a Google account and can skip the next two sections of this chapter. For example, you will already have a Google account if you use the following:

- Core services such as Gmail, Google Talk, Google Calendar, Docs

- Acquired services such as Picasa, YouTube, Google Voice

- Integrated services such as Google Wallet, Blogger, Google Maps

- Desktop services such as iGoogle, Google Desktop, Google SketchUp

If you have acquired a username and password for any of these services, then you already have a Google account. To confirm this, head to Google.com; once there, as shown in Figure 3–1, click the link to the service that you're using and sign in using your login. You will be brought to your Google account! Take the username and password you used here to your Android tablet and sign into your account on your tablet, just like in Figure 3–2.

Figure 3–1. *Google.com sign-in*

Creating a Google Account from Your Tablet

Google makes it really easy to set up an account no matter where you are, no computer required. Since you already have your new tablet in front of you, you might as well tap that "Create account" button, shown in Figure 3–2, and start the party.

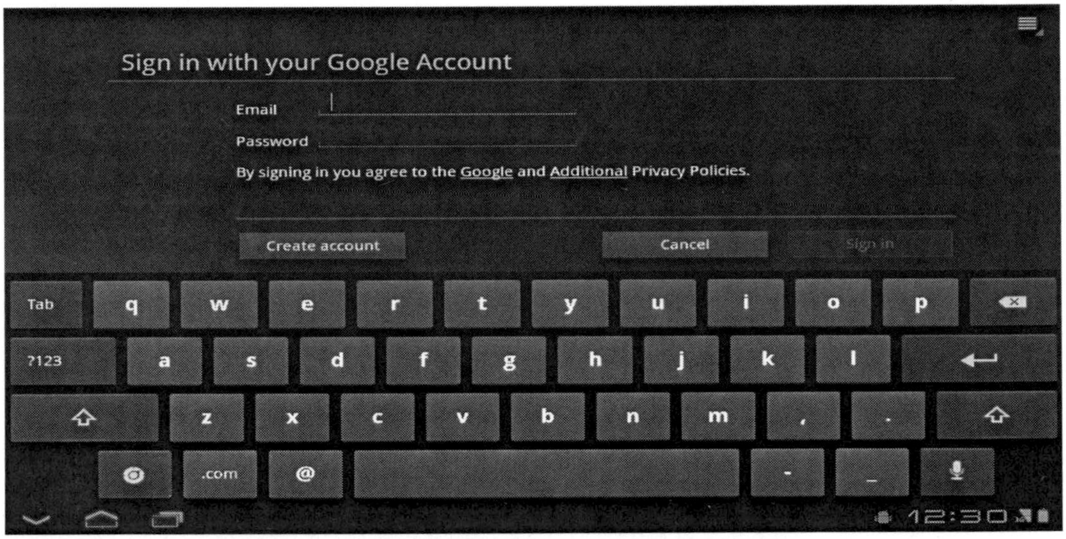

Figure 3–2. *Honeycomb sign-in*

Clicking the "Create account" button causes the "Account setup" screen shown in Figure 3–3 and Figure 3–4 to display. Start this process by entering your first and last names and then choosing a username. Your username can be any name you desire, as long as someone else hasn't already claimed it. The name you choose will also become your new e-mail address; just add "@gmail.com" to the name you choose to form your new address. After you select a username, be sure to click the "Check availability" button. This will make sure that nobody else is currently using that name.

In the event that your desired username is taken, Google will provide you with four alternatives, though you don't have to choose any of them. To check the availability of a different username, simply erase your first choice and start again.

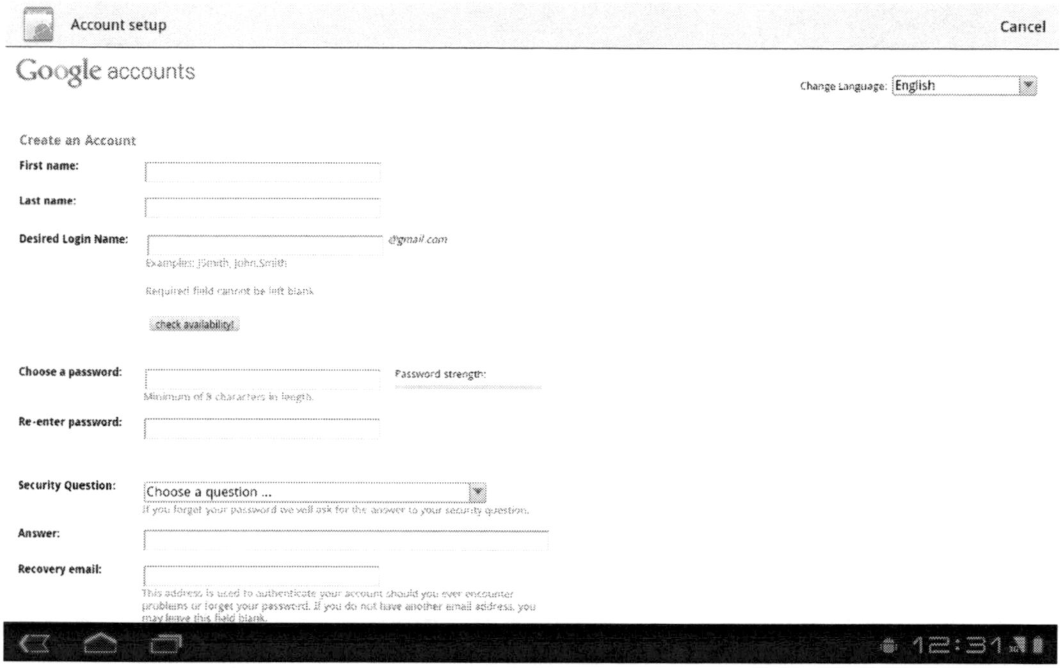

Figure 3–3. *Creating a Google account with Honeycomb*

The security features of your Google account include a password strength gauge, the ability to set a challenge question and answer of your choosing, and an optional recovery e-mail address that you can use to send your password to another e-mail address in case you lose it. Any of these security features can be changed at any time from the Settings app on your tablet.

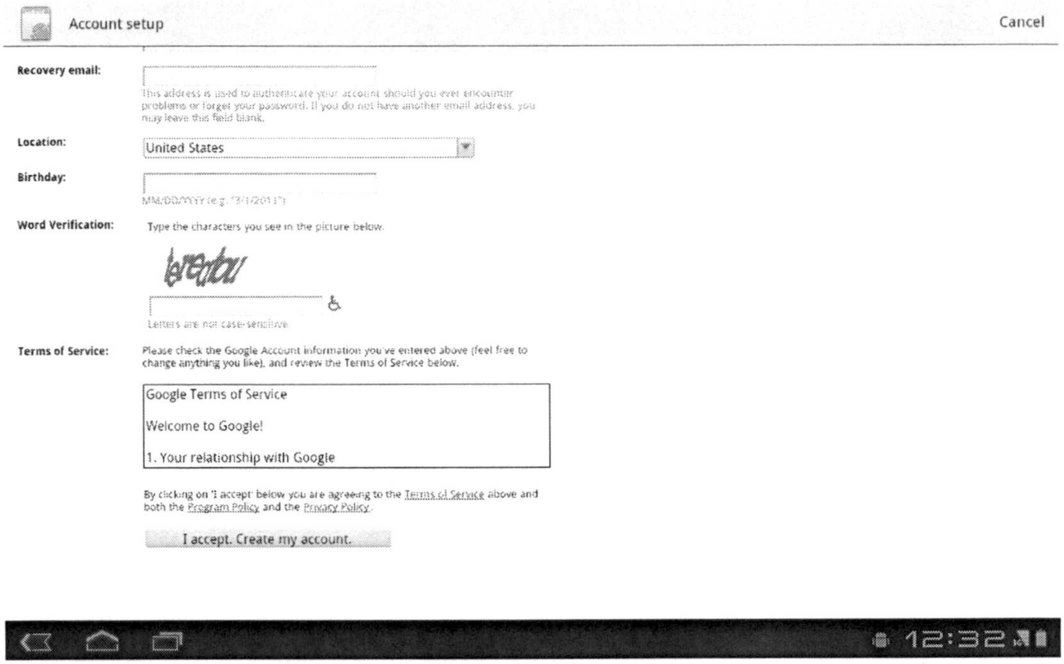

Figure 3–4. *Creating a Google account with Honeycomb (continued)*

The setup page will also ask you to complete its Word Verification field. This feature is one you'll find on most websites that require you to create an account these days; it is a security measure put in place to ensure that a program is not creating false accounts or using stolen information to create an account. Simply type the individual letters you see displayed. If you are having trouble seeing them or understanding them, click the wheelchair button, and the letters will be spoken to you.

Read the terms of service before selecting "I accept" by placing your finger inside the box and "dragging" up. This action will scroll the text in the box, allowing you to read the entire agreement. Once you have read the agreement, touch the "I accept" button on the screen.

Creating an Account on Google.com

If you would rather create your Google account on your desktop or laptop computer, it's just as easy, and you get to use your keyboard!

Grab your browser of choice, head to Google.com, and click the "Sign in" button, as shown in Figure 3–5.

Figure 3–5. *Creating a Google account from a browser*

From here you should see the "Create an account now" link that will direct you to the account creation form, similar to the one you saw on the tablet. Click the link, and you'll see the form displayed in Figure 3–6.

When you create a Google account from your tablet, you are prompted to choose a username, and that username is used both as the login username for your Google account and as the basis for a @gmail.com e-mail address. When you create an account at the Google web site, you gain some flexibility. For example, if you have an e-mail address that is already your address for everything, there is no reason to create a new account that you aren't likely to use, right? When creating a Google account, you can choose to connect your existing e-mail address to it, no matter what kind of e-mail address it is. Should you decide you also would like to set up a Gmail account at the same time, you can select the Gmail link to the left, instead of the "Create an account" link, and you will be taken to a form that will allow you to create your Google account *and* your Gmail account. If you decide to use an existing e-mail address now and create a Gmail account later, this is very easy to do. Nearly all of Google's services are free and can be added to a Google account at any time.

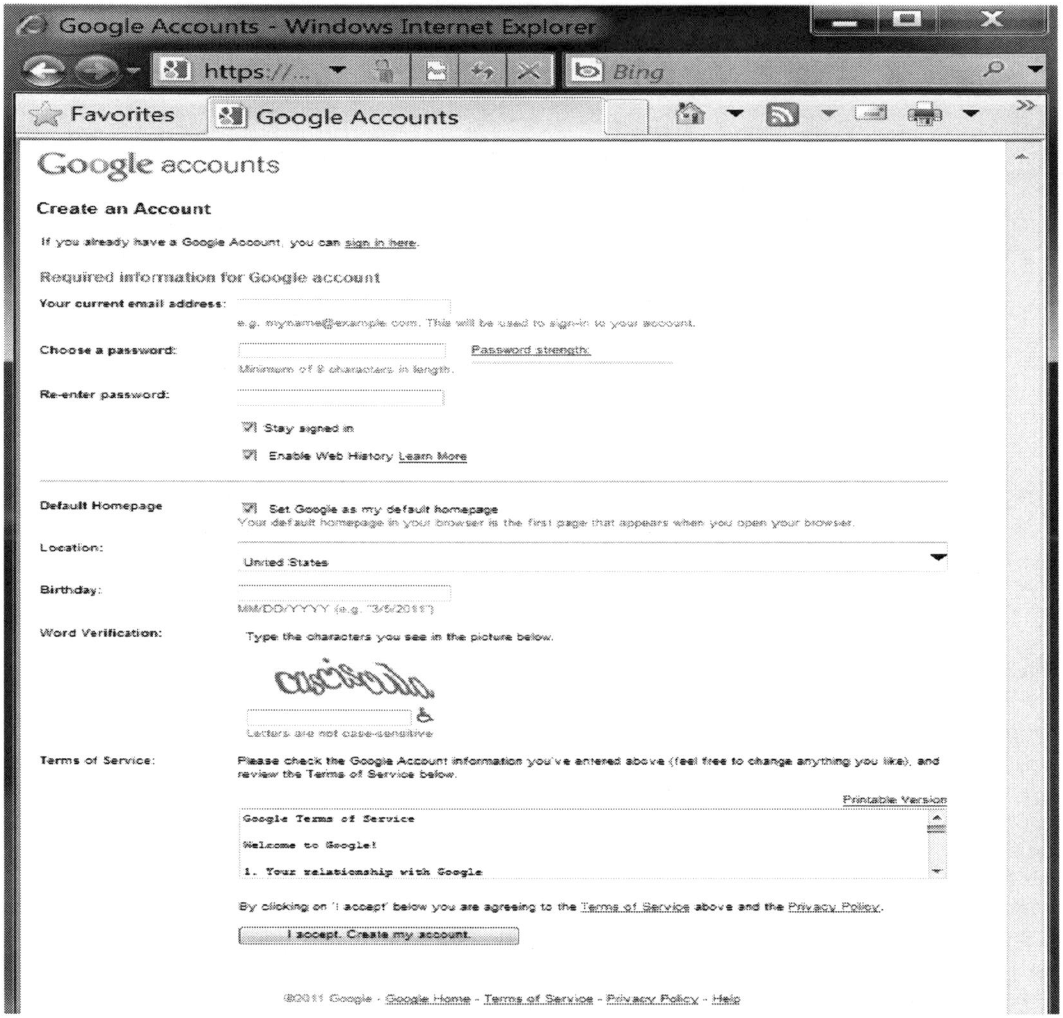

Figure 3–6. *Creating a Google account from a browser (continued)*

Syncing with Your Google Account

Everything you do on your Android tablet can be synced to your Google account and other Google devices you use, such as an Android phone. This includes apps and books you purchase in the Play Store, contacts you have saved in your Gmail or Google Talk accounts, and calendar events. Information that you save inside the apps you install from the Play Store is also stored in your Google account. This gives you the ability to access your personal information from any computer by signing into Google.com or by logging into one of your Android devices.

You will be prompted to activate these synchronization features when you first log in successfully to your Android device, as shown in Figure 3–7.

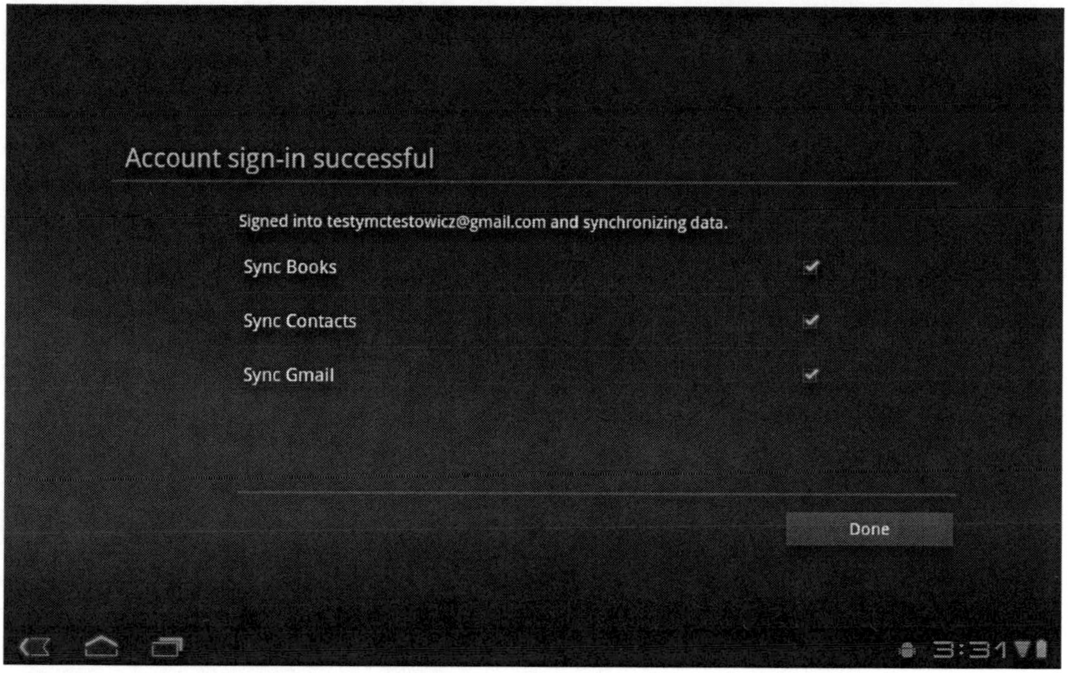

Figure 3–7. *Honeycomb sign-in success screen*

These features can also be controlled at any time in the Settings app, which can be found in My Apps. From Settings, tap the Accounts and Sync tab, and you will be presented with a list of your accounts as well as some general sync settings. Tap the account you want to modify, and you will be presented with your account sync controls, as shown in Figure 3–8.

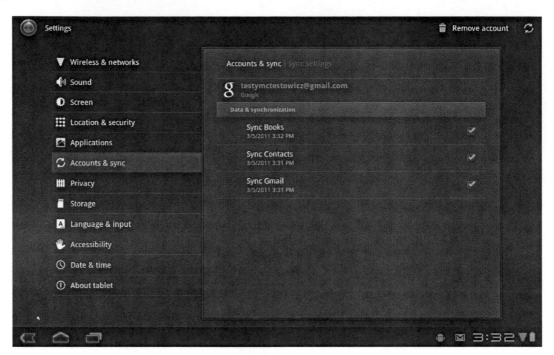

Figure 3–8. *Syncing your Google apps with Honeycomb*

Choosing to sync all your data prevents the unnecessary duplication of tasks. For example, if you read an e-mail on your tablet, wouldn't you want your phone and your computer to know it? If you finish a chapter in that book you've been reading, wouldn't it be easier if all your other devices *knew* to start you at the next chapter when you next logged in? Sync provides this ability across all your Google account devices. If you update a colleague's e-mail address in a meeting, your tablet will already have made the change when you come back to it.

Enabling syncing is also ideal for disaster recovery. Say your home floods or you are in an accident and your tablet is damaged. Because your data is backed up into your Google account, there is no need to be concerned that you have lost any information. When you get your replacement device, simply log back into your Google account, and everything will sync back just the way it was.

Adding Contacts

Every app has the ability to pull information from the contacts stored in your Google account for whatever you may need it for. Maybe chatting on Google Talk, sending an e-mail, sharing a picture...it could be anything. If you have been using some other service to store all your contacts, such as AOL or a client application such as Microsoft Office or ACT!, there are some quick and easy steps for grabbing that list and adding it to your Google account, using either your tablet or another computer. You can also add contacts manually. We'll discuss all these techniques in the next two sections.

Importing Contacts

To add contacts from another service or program to your tablet, you must first export them. Each e-mail service provides the ability to export your contacts to a single file, commonly a comma-separated (CSV) file. Once you have acquired this file, all you need to do is hand off the file to your Google account, and your contacts will be organized and synced across your devices.

If you are using your computer to populate your Google contacts list, you will need to log in to the Gmail account you are using for your tablet and select My Contacts from the left navigation bar. From here you will be presented with several options in a list on the left side (as shown in Figure 3–9). At the bottom of that list you will see Import Contacts. Select it from the list, and the pop-up shown in Figure 3–9 will appear.

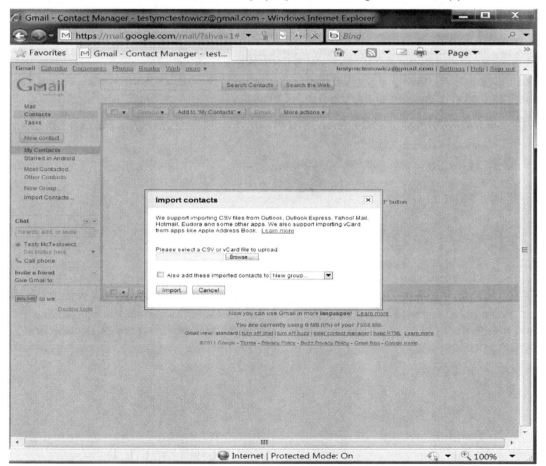

Figure 3–9. Importing contacts to Google.com with a browser

Once you see the "Import contacts" pop-up, click Browse, and locate the contacts file that you created on your computer. (The location of this file will vary based on how you exported it and which service you used to accomplish this task. Common places are the desktop and Downloads folder.) Once you've selected the contact file is, click Import. This will start the sorting and syncing process, which can take several minutes depending on your Internet connection and how many contacts you have. You will see contacts begin to appear on your tablet as they are synced across your Google account. The sync process can take up to an hour, so do not be concerned if certain contacts do not immediately appear.

You may have been able to download your contacts file using the web browser on your tablet, or perhaps you have copied the file to an SD card or transferred the file to your tablet. There are similar steps to importing your contacts from your tablet.

Adding Contacts Manually

The Contacts app, found in My Apps, is the centralized location for all the contact data on your tablet. From here, you can add, edit, remove, and organize your contacts as you see fit. Once you have the opened the Contacts app (shown in Figure 3–10), you will see the menu icon displayed at the top right of the app.

Figure 3–10. *An example of a single contact in the Contacts app*

Once you see the menu options, tap Import/Export (as shown in Figure 3–11) from the list. From here you will browse your tablet for the contacts file. Select the correct file, and the contacts will be synced to your Google account, beginning the organizing and syncing process.

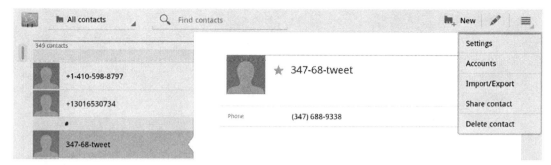

Figure 3–11. *Displaying the Contacts app menu Honeycomb*

So, maybe you have only ten friends, or maybe all of your contacts sync automatically from services like Facebook or Twitter and you need to add only a handful more. Going through the import process will take just as much time as entering in the contacts manually.

In both the computer and tablet versions of your contacts manager, you have the ability to enter a single contact.

When you select New from the top right of the screen in Figure 3–11, you will be presented with a new contact form (as shown in Figure 3–12). This form will create a single contact. All the information you place in this file will be saved to your Google account. You can add a photo of the contact, and if your tablet has a camera, you can also take a picture of the contact from within the file simply by tapping the gray silhouette. Information such as physical a address will be saved as a link to Google Maps where it can be viewed and where directions can be requested.

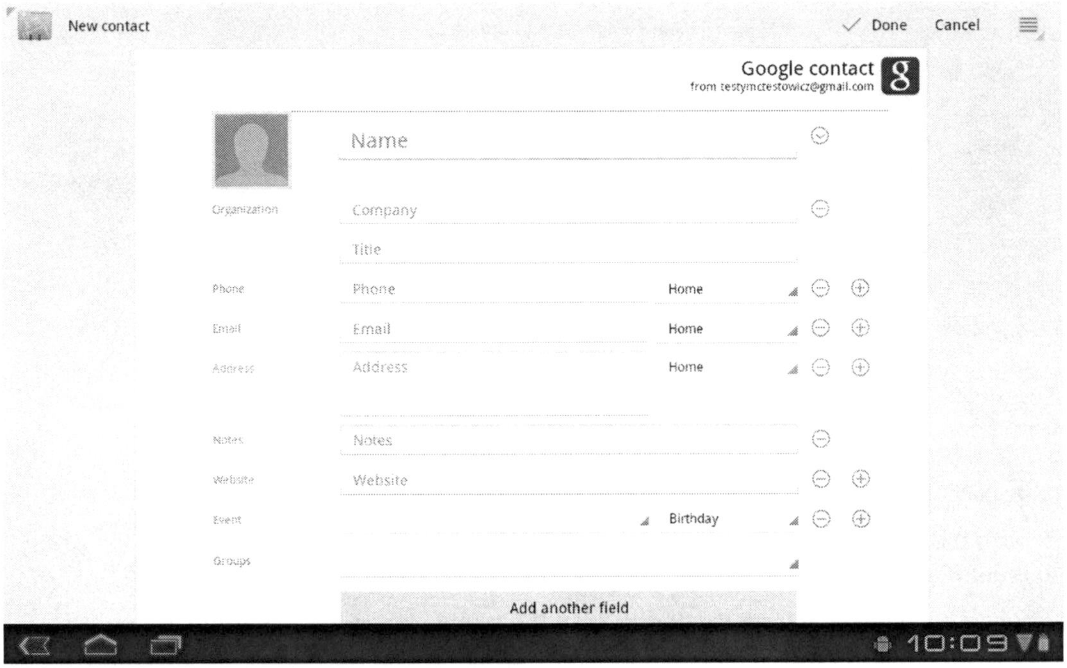

Figure 3–12. *Adding a new contact in Honeycomb*

The contact you create here becomes a dynamic profile of the individual, providing much more information to you than just a name and an e-mail address. Tapping the "Add another field" button will give you the ability to add instant messenger names, nicknames, your relationship to the contact, and much more. Once you are finished, tap the Done check mark, and the contact will be saved to your device and synced to your Google account.

Summary

Your Google account is by far one of the most powerful tools at your disposal on an Android tablet. With it, your information, your preferences, and everything you put into the account is stored online and backed up elsewhere. Having a Google account helps limit the daily minutia of checking e-mail, chatting, or remembering what page you were on to a single task rather than one that must be repeated across devices.

These abilities are far from the limit of the potential of your Google account. On an Android device, your Google account also gives you access to a series of powerful applications that help drive the Android experience. In the next chapter, you will learn about the individual apps that Google has included with its tablets that will give you access to key Google account features, as well as popular Google.com web services.

Chapter 4

Taking Advantage of Google Apps

The most powerful feature in the Android OS is the collection of applications that make up the Google Apps suite. This suite consists of applications that are available only on devices that have been approved by Google, and the process that tablet manufacturers go through in order to have access to this suite is set up by Google to ensure the quality of the device and the dedication of the manufacturer to keep the device updated. Google Apps is essentially the collection of the tools offered by Google on its web site, as well as on the Play Store.

In this chapter, you'll learn how to use the most popular of Google's Android apps to enhance your tablet experience, as well as some tips and tricks to help you get the most out of these apps. Let's get started with Gmail, the application you're likely to use the most.

Gmail

Google's e-mail service is an extremely popular product, second only to the company's iconic search bar. Gmail is used globally on just about every smartphone OS. Like all of Google's apps, Gmail is deeply integrated into Android, allowing you to access it quickly to attach a photo, video, and more. Gmail can be quickly summoned to e-mail a contact or vCard straight from your contacts list and offers all of the same functionality you get from its web-based implementation.

> **NOTE:** Being logged into Gmail occurs automatically after signing into your Google account on your tablet, much like it does on an Android smartphone.

In this section, you'll learn the basics of navigating Gmail, composing an e-mail, and customizing the Gmail experience to your personal tastes. The examples and steps in this chapter are geared for Android 3.0 and newer, but many of these same instructions work on all Android tablets.

Navigate Gmail

From your tablet, you have a couple of ways to get into Gmail. The Gmail icon is located with the other app icons in the app drawer called My Apps. Tap the white envelope with red trim to launch Gmail. Additionally, you can enter Gmail through a notification. If you have a Gmail notification, which would appear as an envelope in your Notifications tray, you can tap that icon and be taken straight to your Gmail Inbox. In this section, you'll learn how to navigate your inbox and e-mails.

Inbox View

Whether you are holding the tablet in portrait or landscape position, the Inbox view will present you with a scrollable list of all the messages in your inbox. It will give enough space to each message to offer you a brief look into the e-mail, as well as the time the message was received and a conversation count per message, in the event that the message you are looking at is one of a thread of messages. This all functions just like the Gmail web site. On your left (as shown in Figure 4–1), a separately scrollable list of your folders is available, allowing you to switch to any folder quickly without leaving this view.

> **NOTE:** Honeycomb users will be able to return to the Inbox view at any time while in the Gmail app simply by tapping the icon shaped like a file box at the top right of the app.

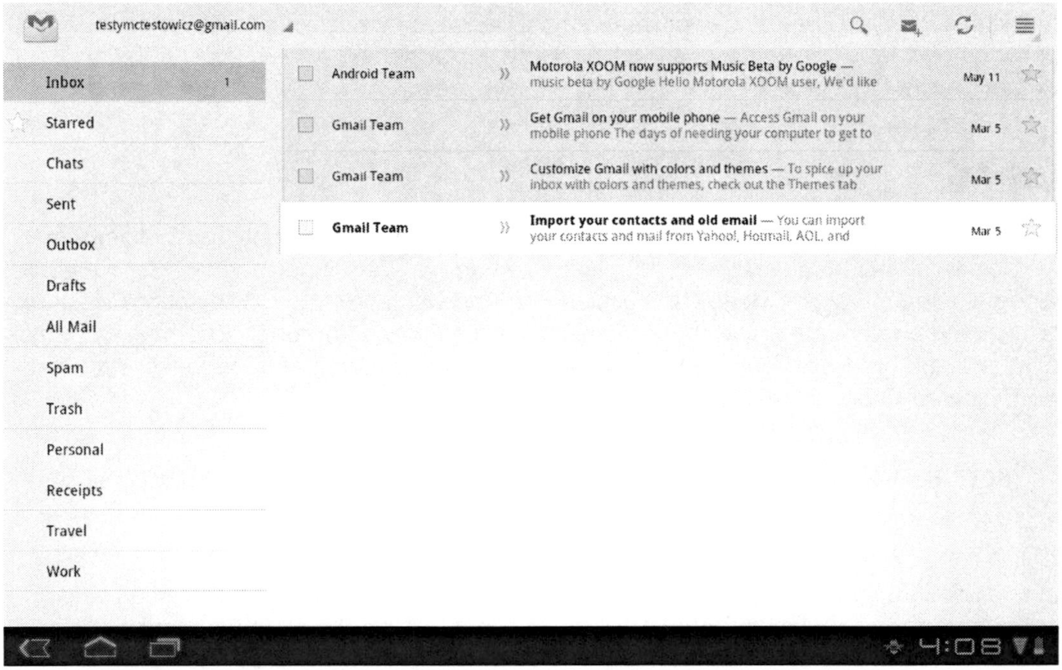

Figure 4–1. *Gmail for Android 3.0 Inbox view*

E-mail View

E-mail view has two different "modes" depending on how you hold the tablet, be it portrait or landscape. For many Android tablets, especially Honeycomb or Android 3.0 and newer devices, landscape is the most common. Once you've selected a message, the left folder navigation slides away, leaving you with a scrollable e-mail and a separately scrollable, but now much thinner, inbox (as shown in Figure 4–2). In portrait view, selecting an e-mail will cause both the inbox and the folders to slide away, leaving the whole space for the e-mail.

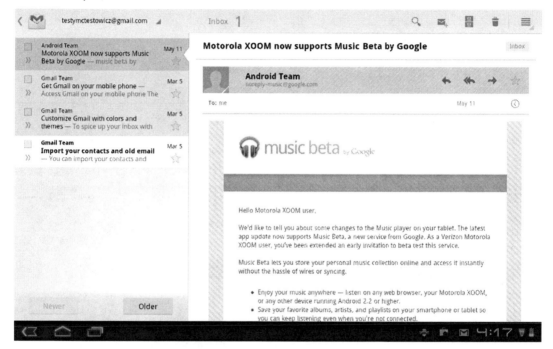

Figure 4–2. *Gmail for Android 3.1 E-mail view*

The Inbox and E-mail views will look the same when you send a new message or reply to an existing one, in that you are only able to interact with the e-mail you are working on. Once you have sent the message, you return to the previous view.

Now that you understand the basics of navigating the Gmail app, you're ready to compose an e-mail.

Compose an E-mail

Before you can compose a message, you need to get yourself to the Gmail Compose screen. There are two ways to navigate to the new message composition screen:

- From within the Gmail app, select the new e-mail icon (the envelope with a plus symbol in front of it, as shown in Figure 4–2).

- From anywhere else, if you are attaching text, pictures, or web site links, tap the Share option in the menu, and select Gmail from the list of sharing options.

Once you've reached this screen, shown in Figure 4–3, you'll be ready to compose a new message.

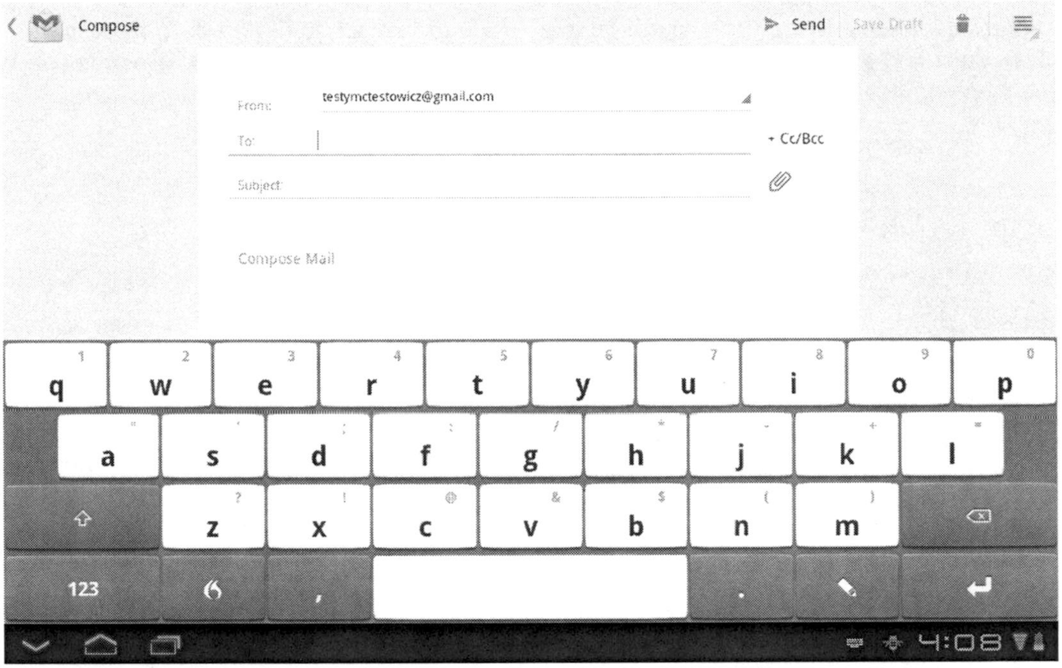

Figure 4–3. *Composing e-mail on Android 3.1*

From the Compose screen, you'll have a few options at your disposal, like those you'd expect to see in any modern e-mail client, such as Outlook Express.

- *To, Cc, and Bcc*: Complete these fields as you would for any other e-mail application you've ever used. All three are tied directly to your Google contacts. If the person you are trying to e-mail is in your contacts list, all you need to do is start typing in their name and the e-mail address will appear. To send a message to multiple recipients, separate the contacts with a comma. To open the Cc and Bcc fields to send a copy or blind copy to a colleague, tap the +Cc/Bcc symbol to the right of the **To** field.

- *Message body*: From the body, you'll simply tap once in the large white box under the To, Cc, and Bcc fields, and your keyboard will appear for you to type your e-mail. Press and hold in a single space, and the Paste function will appear, in case you need to paste anything you may have copied from elsewhere.

- *Attach*: Just like Gmail for your computer, you can attach any image, song, video clip, or URL that is on your tablet to an e-mail. Tap the attach icon (usually a paper clip), and navigate the menu that appears to locate the content you want to attach.

- *Trash*: So, they aren't all winners. You don't like the e-mail you're working on, tap the trash can icon on the top right of the screen, and the message will be deleted, sending you back to the Inbox view. Until you perform another action, you will have an "undo" button at the top of your screen. Tapping undo will send you back to composing your e-mail.

- *Save Draft*: If you are in the middle of a message and need to go do something else, you can save the message as a draft by tapping the Save Draft button next to the trash can. Your drafts are saved to the Drafts folder, which you can access in the inbox. Additionally, if you leave the Gmail app in the middle of writing a message, the app will save the message to the Drafts folder automatically.

- *Send*: When your message is complete, click Send, or if you're interrupted, click Save Draft so you can return to it later.

With that, your e-mails will fly from your tablet to their intended destinations. Plus, all of your folders and drafts are also all on your Gmail.com account, allowing you to move between them seamlessly. There are some features, however, that allow you to customize the experience for your benefit (as seen in Figure 4–4).

Customize Gmail

Just as you can make changes to a traditional e-mail client like Outlook or a web-based client like Gmail on a desktop or laptop computer, the Gmail app has a page of settings for controlling such features as sync frequency, signatures, and some other things to customize your e-mail experience to your needs.

Accessing the settings happens within the app in every version of Android. Simply tap your Menu button within the Gmail app, and the Settings option will appear. Tapping the Settings button will bring you to the Settings panel. If you have multiple accounts loaded on your tablet, select the account you would like to modify from the list on the left (as shown in Figure 4–4).

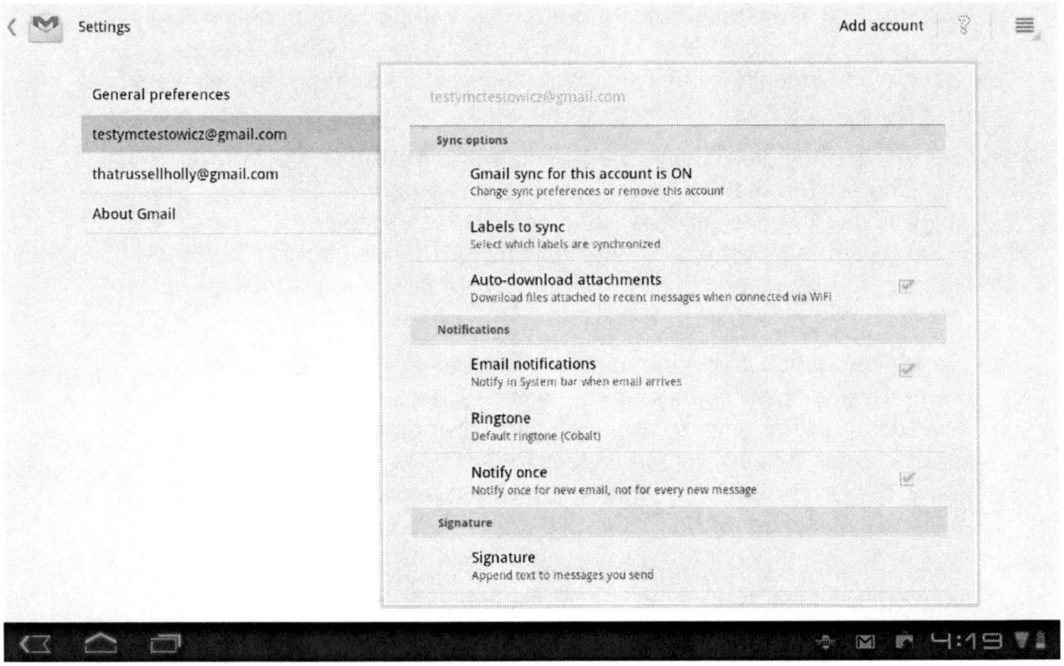

Figure 4–4. *Gmail settings Android 3.1*

On this page, you are able to change the sync options for your account. This includes sync frequency, which you can modify based on personal preference. If you want an e-mail the moment it is sent to you, you can increase the speed at which your account syncs to the device.

> **NOTE:** The more frequently you sync your device to Gmail, the more battery life that is consumed. If you don't receive a lot of e-mail or are unconcerned with how fast it arrives on your device, consider lowering the frequency to conserve battery life.

You can also control which of your labels are synced to your tablet. As you can see in Figure 4–4, you can choose to sync just what is in your inbox, or you can sync everything from your Drafts, Spam, and even Trash folder; this is entirely based on your preference.

By default, your Gmail app is set to notify you every time you receive an e-mail with an icon in the notification bar as well as a preselected ringtone of some kind. These can also be modified on this page, including the ability to either turn off or select whatever ringtone you would like as a notification.

Signatures are another important thing to customize. The Settings page allows you to set your signature, and by default that signature will show up every time you reply to or create a new e-mail.

When used to its fullest extent, Gmail is a powerful and versatile utility, much like its web-based counterpart, and the ability to send an e-mail quickly from virtually anywhere within Android for any reason makes it all the more valuable. Like many of Google's apps, Gmail is accessible via the Share function throughout the operating system. You will find it next to pictures, web sites, text you have copied, and many other places. The Gmail button within share lets you to take whatever you are sharing and attach it to an e-mail.

Gmail.com is used as a portal for just about all of Google's services. Since there are more than a billion active Gmail accounts, it makes good sense that if there were other things to do in Gmail, you'd use them as well. In the next section, you'll learn about Google Talk and how it works on your tablet.

Google Talk

Your "@gmail.com" e-mail address gives you access to all of Google's primary products. Because of this, your Gmail address is also used to create an instant messenger account on Google Talk (shown in Figure 4–5), which is Google's messaging service. Everyone with a Gmail account has a Google Talk login name as well, and there are *lots* of Gmail users, so chances are you know a few people already using Google Talk every day. You can choose not to use this service if you don't want, but like many of Google's other services, it is a great tool on Android tablets because of how deeply integrated it is.

Figure 4–5. *The Google Talk home screen on Android 3.0*

Let's look at how you can use Talk to communicate with colleagues and friends.

There's a pretty good chance that you have used an instant messaging service before. Like Google Talk, most other instant messaging services were built into the service that spawned them. For example, Yahoo! Messenger, AOL Instant Messenger (AIM), and Windows Live Messenger were not originally the stand-alone services they are today. Google's service offers many of the same features and comes built into the Gmail service. This app is an extension of that service, offering a great deal of the same functionality.

Add Some Friends

If you've never used Google Talk before, you're going to want some friends. The Google Talk app is in your My Apps drawer, shaped like a white speech bubble with *TALK* written across it in blue. At the top right of the app you will see the silhouette of a person with a plus sign underneath. Tapping that icon will prompt a pop-up, asking you to invite a friend to chat (as shown in Figure 4–6). All you need to know to invite a friend is their Google Talk address, which is almost always their Gmail address.

> **NOTE:** Google's business services have made Google Talk available to companies that would rather use their own e-mail address, not one that ends in "@gmail.com." Because of this, some of your Google Talk friends might not use their Gmail accounts for Google Talk.

Figure 4–6. *Google Talk chat invite*

Set Your Status Message

Now that you have some friends, let them know what is going on in your world through a status message. This will appear next to your name any time any of your friends see you online. These messages are accompanied by an availability icon, which comes in green for Available and red for Not Available or Busy. Additionally, if your availability is set to green and you are inactive for more than an hour, the status icon will turn orange to signify that you're not actively using Google Talk. To add a status, tap the gray box with the pencil icon, and fill in your status using the virtual keyboard that will pop up. After you've set a status, you can choose whether you are available, and that information will be displayed on your friends list of anyone who you have invited to use Google Talk with you.

Chat with a Friend

The Google Talk app is set up so that you always have access to your list of friends on the left side of the screen, and that alphabetical list is scrollable, in case you have a lot of friends. When you tap any of your friends, you are initiating a chat with them. The window to the right will change, prompting you to send a message to your friend. When you have an active chat going on with a friend, their name and icon are brought to the top of your friends list. If you have multiple conversations going on with friends, they will all be at the top, making it easy to switch back and forth in conversations. To terminate a conversation, tap the X in the top right of the chat window, and their name will return to the alphabetical spot in line.

Video Chat with a Friend

A feature that is growing in popularity daily with Android tablets is the ability to video chat with your friends. What makes video chat unique in Google Talk is that you can do so with anyone who has a Google Talk account. If they are on a computer, a supported Android phone, or another tablet, you can chat with them using the camera and microphone on your tablet (as shown in Figure 4–7). Video chat is available to anyone on a Wi-Fi connection, but video chat over 3G or 4G will depend on your carrier.

Figure 4–7. *Google Talk video chat*

As you look at your friends list, your friends that are ready for video chat will have a green camera as their status icon, instead of a green circle. Tap the user you want to start a video chat with on the right side of your chat window. As of right now, you can video chat with only one person at a time. Once you tap the camera, Google Talk will "call" the person you want to chat with, and once they answer, the video chat session will begin. As with a normal chat session, tap the X in the right corner to terminate it.

Customize Your Settings

Tap that Menu button in the app, and Settings will appear. Tap Settings, and the Settings page will appear, allowing you to customize your chat experience. If you have multiple Google Talk accounts signed in, you can change individual settings for each account by tapping the account you want to change.

If you don't plan to use Google Talk, you can remove the default setting "Sign in automatically" with a tap, and Google Talk will run only when you open the app from the My Apps menu. You can also choose to change your icon from the green circle or camera to a mobile indicator (as shown in Figure 4–8), letting everyone know you are on a mobile device.

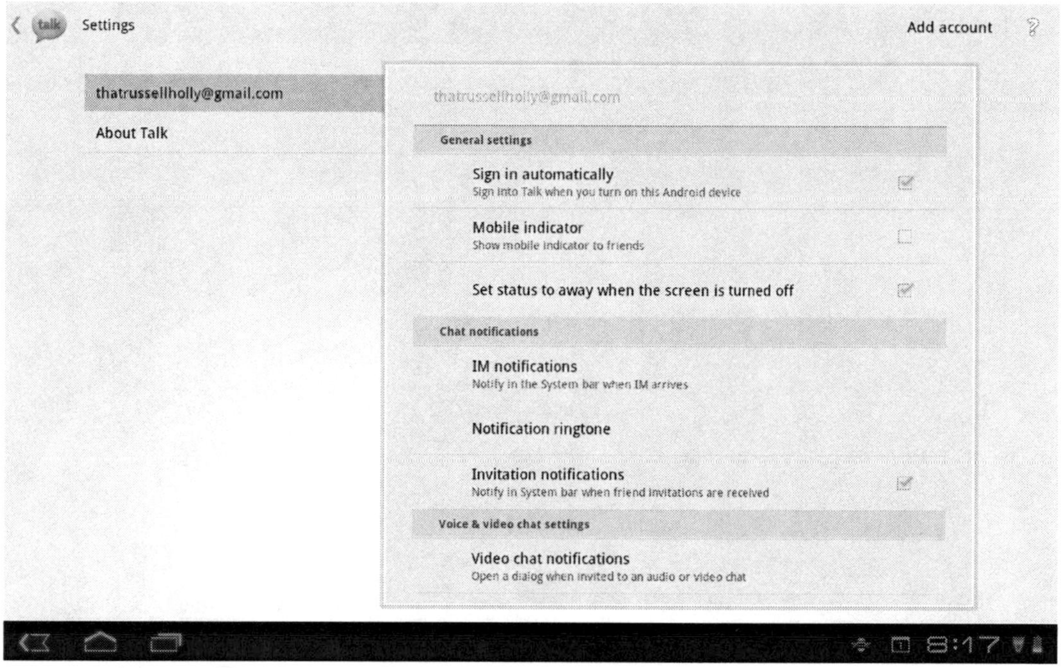

Figure 4–8. *Google Talk settings*

Notification settings are available here, if you would like to have a separate ringtone for Google Talk or if you are not interested in the tablet vibrating when you get a message. You can set the ringtone to any of the available notification tones or turn the sound off entirely for this app.

Video chat settings allow you to control how you receive new video chats, including what ringtone you would like to hear when someone "calls" you via video chat. By default, the app is configured to pop up on the screen when there is an incoming chat and allow you to answer it immediately without leaving whatever app you are currently in.

Google Talk is always ready and waiting for you to communicate with your friends in whatever way you choose, and if you choose, the app is always running in the background, so your friends can reach you as long as you are near your tablet.

Google Maps

It certainly never occurred to me that my Android tablet could replace my GPS when I first started using it, but Google has included all the bits necessary to do so! Or, if you'd just like a nice map application to look for local restaurants, to plan a trip, or even to see where your friends are, Google Maps can do that too. In fact, everything you can do on the Google Maps web site can be done on the tablet, making it a very powerful utility for any user (Figure 4–9).

Figure 4–9. *Google Maps on Android 3.1*

Find Locations on a Map

If you aren't familiar with MultiTouch screens, navigating Google Maps will be a new experience for you. The first time you open this app, you see a map of the world. If you would like to zoom into a specific point on the map, a few options are available to you. If you know where you want to go, you can just type in the address or location in the search bar by tapping the magnifying glass where it says *Search Maps* in the top left (as shown in Figure 4–9). If you aren't quite sure where you want to go, you can double-tap any place on the map, and it will zoom in some to that position. You can continue to double-tap until you get where you want to go. Finally, you can pinch the screen to zoom in where you want to go. Place two fingers on the screen where you want to go and expand your fingers on the glass. As you expand your fingers, the map will zoom in.

Add Map Info with Layers

As you use a map, Google lets you add information to the display that could be helpful to you in your travels. These add-ons are provided by layers, like the transparent overlays used in traditional anatomy texts or engineering diagrams. Each layer contains an entirely different kind of information, and layers can be combined to give you even more. You can access your layers by tapping the icon to the top right that looks like three pieces of paper in a stack. Figure 4–10 shows what's available.

Figure 4–10. *Layers in Google Maps*

■ *Traffic*: When active, this layer will provide a color overlay on major roads to give you a sense of how the traffic is on these roads. The overlay can be in either green, yellow, red, or gray depending on the severity of the traffic, with gray being "unknown."

■ *Satellite*: Photos taken from space will replace the vector images that make up the default map, giving you a real-life view of the world around you.

■ *Terrain*: A topographical map overlays the original images, giving the map depth for valleys, mountains, and more. The Terrain layer and the Satellite layer can't be on at the same time.

■ *Wikipedia*: Historical landmarks, famous locations, and more that are stored at Wikipedia.com are overlaid onto the map. Selecting any of the individual items that appear on the map will pop up a brief chunk of the Wikipedia article associated with it, followed by a link to the full article. This layer is found under the More Layers button at the bottom of the Layers list.

■ *Transit Lines*: Bus and train stations become highlighted in the map, and selecting these will give you a pop-up with arrival and departure times, if they are available. This layer is found under the More Layers button at the bottom of the Layers list.

As much fun as it is to play with the map all day, you're probably going to want to use it to be somewhat productive. The best way to do that is to use the app to look up directions to and from anywhere.

Get Directions

If you decided to navigate the app by searching for an address, then the result you would have received is a dot on the map with the address above it in a bubble. If you tap that bubble, a menu will pop up with options for sharing the location, searching for locations nearby, and finding your way there. The Directions and Navigation icon, a diamond icon with a right turn symbol in the middle, will prompt you to select how you would like to arrive at this destination when you tap it. You can choose to get spoken turn-by-turn navigation to the location, or you can just get directions.

Tapping Get Directions will prompt you to either navigate to that location from a starting address of your choosing or use your current location via GPS. Once you have provided this information, Google Maps will zip back to the starting point of your trip and show you step-by-step directions on the map, guided by a highlighted line. To the left you will also see each step of the directions in a scrollable list, and if you tap any of the individual directions, the map will zip to that point in the trip (as shown in Figure 4–11). When you've reached your destination, simply tap the X in the top right of the directions, and it will go away.

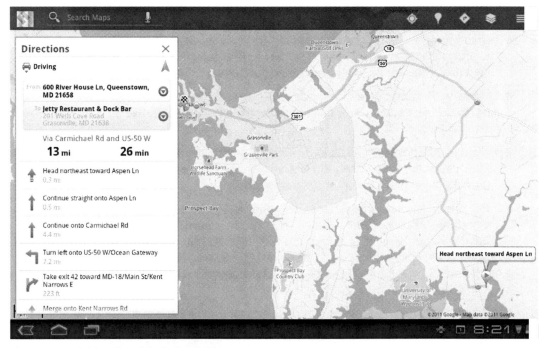

Figure 4–11. *Driving directions in Google Maps*

Having a list of directions is a great way to map out where you are going, but you also have the ability to have the directions spoken to you one turn at a time as you drive or walk to your destination.

Find Your Way with Navigation

Turn-by-turn navigation is one of the other options you can choose when trying to get to a searched location in Google Maps. Tap Driving Navigation or Walking Navigation, and the Navigation app will launch and begin offering you turn-by-turn directions to your location.

Driving Directions in Navigation looks very similar to what you get with many other GPS devices. Once you have selected Driving Navigation, you are presented with a large blue triangle that will travel with you on your trip. As you approach turns, the turn-by-turn navigation will sound out the next step in the trip. During this mode, you can use your fingers to slide in any direction on the map, be it to check out the next step in directions or see what the traffic situation is. When you arrive at your destination, you will be prompted to either enter a new location or exit the navigation. Walking directions work in the same way; only Google Navigation will give you directions from the sidewalk, including the best places to cross roads. Put together, your tablet is going to be able to get you anywhere.

Lots of people use Google Maps every day, so Google created a tool to allow you to see where your friends are on the map. That service is called Google Latitude.

Locate Friends with Latitude

Google offers a system where anybody using its Maps system connected to a Gmail account has the ability to see each other on the map if they request the ability to see each other. The service is called Latitude. It's 100 percent opt-in. No one can see you unless you explicitly give permission for it. You also have the ability to ask others to show you their latitude, and if they agree, you can see their location. Once Latitude is shared with someone else, you can see them on your map by activating the Latitude filter (as shown in Figure 4–12).

Figure 4-12. *Google Latitude*

Latitude will display someone's location based on the last time they had their GPS on in their device. Additionally, you have the ability to constantly monitor someone with their GPS on. For example, if you have given someone directions to a location and are checking to see whether they are making the correct turns, Latitude will do that for you. Tap the Latitude bar on the right of the map, and select a friend from the list. Select the Map icon, and the app will zoom you to wherever their location is on the map.

Google Maps provides a complete GPS solution, social networking savvy, and the wealth of Google's global resources in a single app, making it one of the most powerful tools on your tablet.

Google Maps has widely been hailed as one of the greatest navigation tools on the Play Store today, and it's free with every Android tablet or phone. The service has replaced stand-alone GPS devices for countless users, and it's this very feature that has caused many tablet manufacturers to offer an in-car mount for their devices. In the next section, you'll learn about Google's video watching and sharing app, YouTube.

YouTube

Google didn't invent YouTube, but Google did buy the company a few years ago and since then has worked closely with the original inventors to turn it into the massive video clip library it is today. For tablets, Google has implemented a user interface that makes it easy to search for new videos, watch your favorites, and upload new videos with ease.

YouTube is a stand-alone video watching and sharing service that Google purchased to replace its own Google Videos service. Since then, YouTube has permeated itself into every facet of Google's services. E-mails with YouTube videos in them can be watched right from the e-mail, without the need to redirect you anywhere or take you away from what you were doing. In this section, you'll learn all about how Google put the power of YouTube into an app for you to enjoy and share videos from wherever you are.

Check Out the Wall

When you first load the YouTube app, you are presented with a full screen of videos, known as the Wall, that are currently being watched across the Internet (as shown in Figure 4–13). Most of the videos on this Wall will never be the same any two times you load the application, since YouTube is used by millions around the world 24/7. As you use YouTube, the app will change the items on the Wall for you to include recommendations based on content you have already watched. This is scrollable as well; just drag your finger from right to left on the Wall, and it will rotate, exposing even more videos for you to watch.

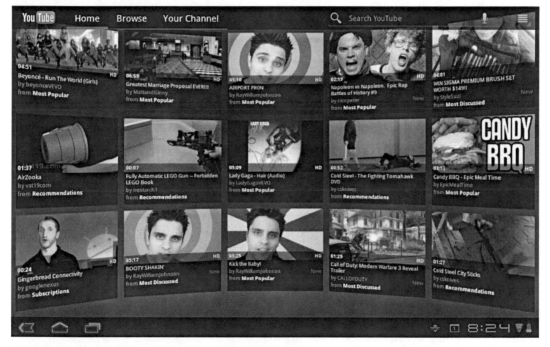

Figure 4–13. *YouTube app on Android 3.1, showing the Wall*

Searching YouTube, in case what you are looking for is not on the Wall, is easy as well. The top right of the app has the standard Google magnifying glass, labeled Search YouTube. Type your search into this bar, and you will be taken immediately to any search results YouTube has for you. As you continue to use this app, your searches will be saved, allowing you to quickly return to something you have previously looked for.

If you watch a lot of YouTube videos, you'll probably spend a lot of time on the Wall. If you are more of the video maker than video watcher, then Your Channel is probably where you will spend most of your time.

Store Videos

YouTube gives you for free a place of your very own to store any videos you have made and want to share with the world. Maybe you've recorded something using the camera on your tablet, or maybe you've used one of the many apps in the Play Store that will help you make videos; you can now upload them quickly and easily. Access Your Channel from the Wall by pressing the tab on the top left of the app. Once there, the left panel will appear with options for you to navigate your existing videos or upload a new one (see Figure 4–14).

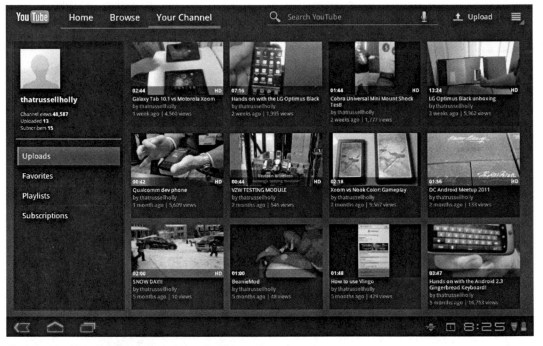

Figure 4–14. *Your channel in Android 3.1 YouTube app*

The Upload button, located on the top right of this page, will help you search your tablet for the video you want to upload. If you are inside another app, for the purposes of making a video, the Share button in those apps will have a YouTube option. Selecting that option will begin the upload process to your YouTube account.

If YouTube isn't new to you and you already have a channel of your own, you can share your videos, even freshly uploaded ones, with your friends and fans with the Share function.

Share Videos

When you already have a video in Your Channel, YouTube wants you to be able to share it with the world. That's why there's a Share button. Choose any of the videos in Your Channel to pull up a detailed view of the video. At the top right of your video you will see the Share button. Tapping that button will bring up a list of all the ways your tablet currently knows to share this video (as shown in Figure 4–15). Gmail, if you'd like to e-mail the link to someone, or Facebook? Bluetooth, Dropbox, Twitter, anything that is supported within Android to share this video will be available. The list of ways you can share a video grows with each new app you install.

Figure 4–15. *Share function in YouTube app*

YouTube is a great video utility, and the ability to quickly share your videos with anyone makes it a great tool for Android tablets not only to create video but also to watch video on the larger screen. Having a camera on your tablet allows you to capture life as it happens and quickly push it to YouTube to share with the world. In the next section, you'll learn how Google took its first and most powerful product, Search, and wove it into the entirety of Android.

Search

Google is, first and foremost, a search company. Because of this, it knows a thing or two about how we like to search for things. Each of the apps you've seen in this chapter provides a way for you to search for something within the app, but what happens when you're not sure exactly where the desired item is to be found on your device? Google solved this problem by allowing you to search your whole tablet from its home screen, as shown in Figure 4–16.

Search Your Tablet with the Keypad

At the top left of your home screen, look for Google's iconic magnifying glass. Tap the icon to bring up your keyboard and type in your search request. As you type, the home screen will disappear and be replaced with potential search results for the Web on the left and potential search results on your tablet to the right (as shown in Figure 4–16). These results will change and become more accurate the more letters you type in, until you locate the result you want. If you select a web result from the left, you will be taken to the browser, where you'll be shown the results as if you had searched on Google.com. The results on the right will be everything from the names of apps to contacts to even names of files or pictures stored on the device. Depending on the type of result, you will be taken to the information you were looking for, or the app you were looking for will launch.

Figure 4–16. *Search in Android 3.1*

Search Your Tablet with Spoken Words

Searching with the search bar is impressive, but what if you don't know how it's spelled, or maybe you're just busy? In almost every place on your tablet that you see the magnifying glass, the microphone is usually not far away. Tapping the mike instead of the magnifying glass will pop up the voice search box. You will be prompted by the pop-up when it is ready to listen to your request, as shown in Figure 4–17. Speak clearly, and when you are finished, Google will translate your request into text and show you the search results. This is just as powerful as the search results, including the ability to launch apps. Want the browser? Tap the microphone and just say the word *Browser*, and a moment later the app will load.

Figure 4–17. *Voice search in Android 3.1*

Search is very powerful on your Android tablet, and thanks to Google, it gets better every day. More languages, more content, and faster delivery of results are always being added to the app, as expected of a company whose primary function is search.

Summary

All of the Google Apps are remarkable versions of their original browser-based relatives. Their usefulness on the tablet makes them some of the most commonly used apps on any tablet. There is, however, another app that Google puts on tablets that you simply can't do without. You can create content with YouTube and Gmail, keep yourself from getting lost with Google Maps, and talk to any of a billion possible friends in Google Talk. All of these apps, right down to the search function, are deeply integrated into Android. This is by far your tablet's most useful set of features, especially if you were already using even one of these products.

In the next chapter, you will learn about the Android Play Store and how to use it to supercharge your Android tablet with the latest in applications made by developers around the world.

Chapter 5

The Play Store

Google includes a variety of powerful and useful utilities and apps with its Android OS. Like everything else on the Internet, however, there's no way even the horde of brains at Google can think of everything. No matter how clever you are, there's a good chance there's someone on the Internet who either is more clever or possesses greater resources to develop something great. With that in mind, Google built the tools necessary for anyone to write and sell apps for Android, and it built a secure place where users can locate and purchase them.

This service is called the Play Store. In this chapter, you will learn how to use the Play Store to search for, purchase, and install not just Android apps but also Google books, movies, and music as well.

Finding and Using Android Apps

On your tablet, the Play Store can be identified quickly by its icon: the image of a white shopping bag with green handles and an Android peeking from the right corner is one that is universal across all Android devices. Typically, you will find the Play Store on your device's home screen. However, like all apps, you can also find the Play Store in your app drawer. Locate the Play Store icon on your device and tap once to open the Store.

> **NOTE:** Honeycomb users can also find a shortcut to the Play Store in Apps. The shopping bag icon is always in the top right of your app drawer, though this version of the icon is much smaller and all white with a black Android in the corner

The Play Store home page, shown in Figure 5–1, is a snapshot of some of the activity going on in the Market today. This page will frequently change with new apps, movies, music, and books as the Store cycles through them. If you take your finger and swipe from the bottom of the screen to the top, you will see all of the activity currently going on within the Store. The landing categories to the left will take you to the sections of the Store you want to go to depending on the content you want. From here, tap the Apps tab.

Figure 5–1. *The Honeycomb Play Store home page*

The Apps tab is the central location for the more than 200,000 apps available in the Play Store. The Featured panel for Apps has a selection of editors' choice and staff-picked apps that will change frequently. When you swipe your finger from the left to the right on the screen, you are shown a list of categories to make it easy for you to browse for a specific kind of app. If you swipe from the right to the left on the screen, you are shown a larger list of staff picks for apps that are optimized for tablets.

If browsing more than 200,000 apps by category really isn't your thing, the search giant offers you a version of the tool that made them famous: a search bar. Located overtop the large sliding banner, the search bar lets you quickly navigate the Store by just entering a name or keyword (or two or three) for whatever you are looking for into the search bar (as shown in Figure 5–2). The Play Store search bar will give you results based on description and app name. This way, if you are searching for a specific app or if you are just looking for apps that perform a specific task, your search results will be diverse.

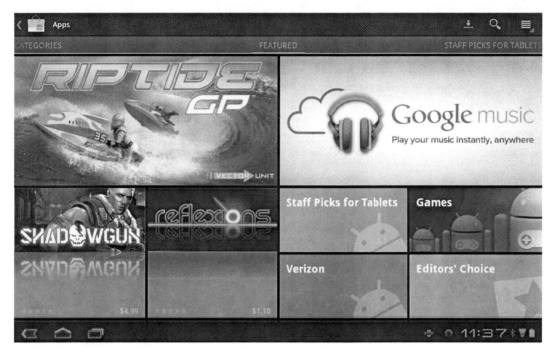

Figure 5–2. *Category view in the Honeycomb Store*

Choosing an App

When you have found an app you think you might like, tap it, and you are taken to that apps product page. This page offers you a description of the features within the app, as well as screenshots of what the app looks like and reviews that have been given by other users of the app.

The first thing you see on this page, to the left of the screen, is the app icon, the price of the app, and its rating. Underneath that you will see what version of the app you are looking at, as well as the size of the app and the total number of downloads since the app has been on the Store, as shown in Figure 5–3. The size of the app can often help you decide when you want to install the app. If it is a large app (for example, 20 to 30 megabytes), it make take some time to install the app if you are in an area with a poor data connection. Additionally, if you are limited to a certain amount of mobile data every month, you may consider waiting until you are on a Wi-Fi network to install large apps, to save your data.

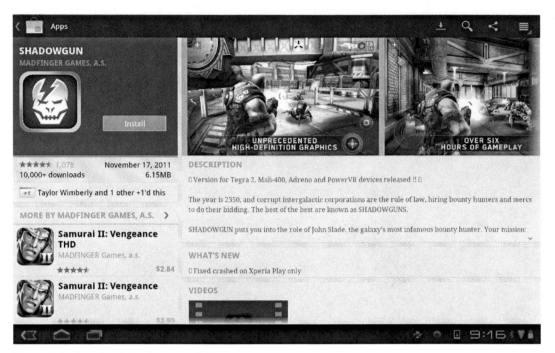

Figure 5–3. *App view in the Honeycomb Store*

To the right of this information you will see a description of the app, as provided by the developer of the app. This will usually include features, benefits, and any other useful information that may help you decide to install the app. Most apps that have been in the Store for a little while take advantage of the "What's New" section beneath the description to discuss new features or to announce they have fixed errors that had previously been found in the app. This way, if you have used an app in the past but decided to replace it with an app that proved more functional, you can choose to quickly see whether an app has improved since you last used it. All of this is shown in Figure 5–3.

Screenshots allow users to get a quick idea of what the app will look like on their device. For games, it's a quick way to show off how good the graphics look, and for other apps it's a great way to show off features. The Screens section of this page scrolls from left to right, revealing a variety of screens. With this feature, app developers can show off their product and help you decide just how worth it the app is to you (as shown in Figure 5–3).

The best way to get a feel for how the app works is in the reviews. The Play Store allows any user who has installed an app to rate and review the app. These reviews are not controlled by the developer of the app, unless someone says something completely off-base, in which case the developer can flag it for Google to take a look and decide whether to remove it. This means that the information here is raw, unedited, and true. Rated from one to five stars, with the combined total of the rating being shown at the top of the screen, app developers need to work hard to make users happy (as shown in Figure 5–4). The reviews in this section are typically on a couple of sentences, but users are able to write quite a bit if they choose to do so.

If you are interested in seeing some information about the developer, such as their web site, or if you would like to contact the developer via e-mail, these options are available at the bottom of every product page, as well as a snapshot of some related apps, just in case you did not find quite what you were looking for on this product page or you want to see what competing apps are offering. If you've decided this is the app for you, it's time to install it!

Installing an App

From the product page, the Install button is in the gray box in the top-left corner, right under the price. If the app costs money, the icon will be labeled Buy. If not, it will be labeled Install. Choosing to buy an app will open a pop-up, prompting you to pay for the app. The top right of this pop-up will say "Add card" if you've never used it. Tapping this will start the process of adding your credit card to Google Checkout.

Figure 5–4. *Purchasing a app on App Honeycomb Store*

Google Wallet is a service that allows you to make purchases all over the Internet in as few clicks as possible, while using a secure payment method. Google has made it easy for existing Google Wallet users to tap OK, confirm that they want to make the purchase, and complete the transaction, as shown in Figure 5–4. For users who have never used Google Wallet, a form will appear for you to add your credit card information into Google Wallet to complete the transaction (as shown in Figure 5–5). If you choose, you can tell Google Wallet to save the card for future transactions, or you can repeat this process every time you want to make a purchase. Once you have selected your payment method in Google Checkout, you will be brought back to the app purchase pop-up.

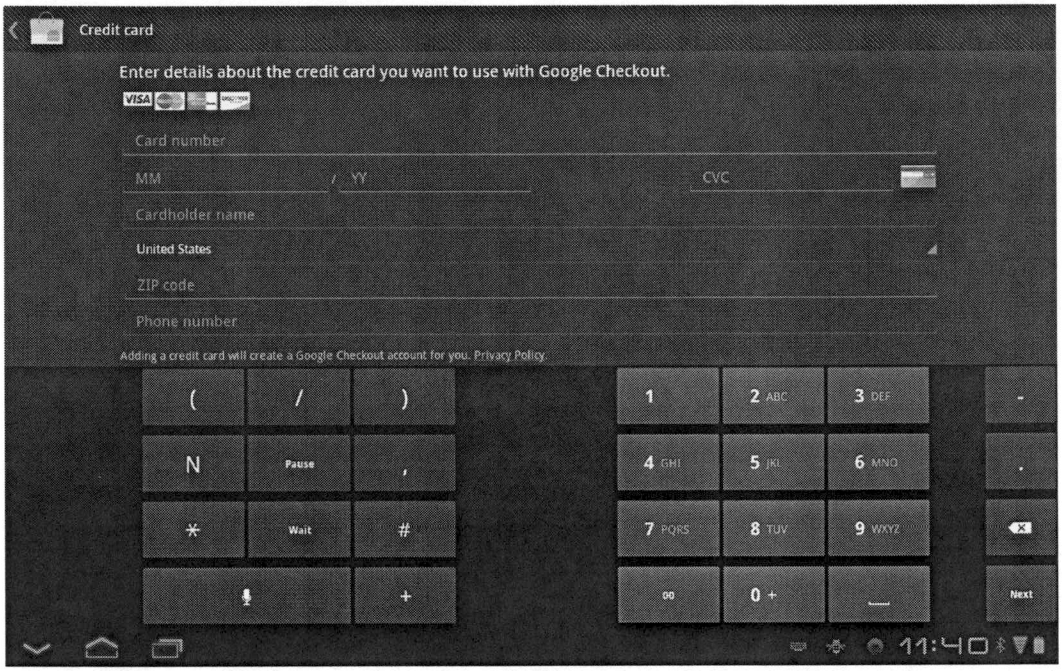

Figure 5–5. *Adding a credit card in Honeycomb Store*

From here you are given some security information. Should an app require the use of any part of your device, you will be informed on this screen, as shown in Figure 5–5. Apps can request the use of resources such as storage on your tablet or a connection to the Internet, or they can request the use of things such as your contacts, your location, and more. Applications must tell you what they have access to, labeled under "This application has access to." Google's app guidelines make sure that app developers are unable to save any of this information; they can access it just temporarily. Make sure you review this information, in case the app you want requires a constant Internet connection or if it needs to access your location in order to function correctly.

Once you have looked the security information over, all you need to do it tap the OK button, and your app will begin to download and then install. Depending on the size of the app and the speed of you Internet connection, this should happen pretty quickly. When finished, you will be redirected to My Apps in the Store, where you will see your new app among the apps that you have already installed (as shown in Figure 5–6). From here, you can tap Open, which has now appeared next to the details, and continue to use your app. Additionally, the app icon will now be in your app drawer.

Updating an App

As you continue to install apps, developers will not only make new ones but also give their existing apps new features. When a developer has new features to add to an app, you will get a notification that an update to one of your apps is available. These updates come to you as soon as the developer pushes the update to the Store. When you see this notification, just tap it and you will be taken to the My Apps section of the Android Store. If an update is available for an app, you will see a new button on the app page. The Update button will appear under the Open button. When you tap this button, the app update will download and install. If this update affects how the app interacts with your device, you will be presented with a new list of Security notifications to let you know what the app will have access to.

Figure 5–6. *My Apps view, app update Honeycomb Store*

If you have a lot of apps, it can be somewhat time consuming to individually update each one as a new update becomes available. To make this easier for you, Google has added an "Allow automatic updating" check box for each of your installed apps, as shown in Figure 5–6. This will allows updates that do not request new functions to install automatically as they become available. If an app is requesting to use new parts of your tablet, you will still need to approve these changes manually.

Submit a Review

Although it is never a requirement, you have the ability to leave feedback on your experiences with anything in the Android Market. This feedback is sent back to the publisher and is available for everyone who uses the Android Market to see. Regardless of how positive or negative your experience, leaving feedback is beneficial for everyone. When you are trying to decide which app to install to accomplish a task, it is often a great tool at your disposal to check the reviews for those apps to see how others enjoyed their experience.

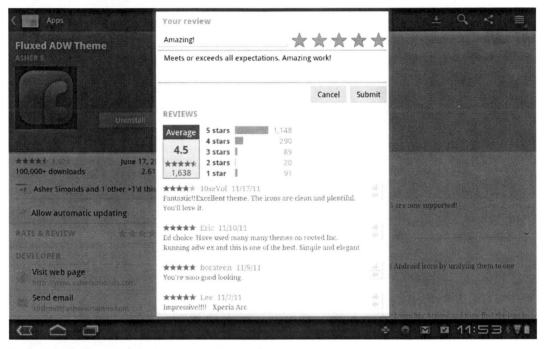

Figure 5–7. *Rating and reviewing an app in the Android Store*

The detailed view of everything in the Play Store has a Rate and Review button on the middle of the left side of the screen. Tap this to open the Review submission screen, as shown in Figure 5–7. From here you can rate every app from one star to five stares and leave commentary on your experience. Once you have finished, tap the submit button and the feedback will be available for everyone on the Play Store to see.

What makes the Play Store especially functional is that all of this is done from the tablet. There is no need to connect it to your computer for any of this, and the applications that you have paid for are saved to your account, so if you ever move to a new device, those apps will be right there waiting for you. If you would rather use a computer, however, that option is also available to you, as you'll learn in the next section.

Using the Play Store on the Web

With any web browser, including the one on your computer, you can also to remotely install and manage your Android apps on any Android device you own. From any browser, on any device, go to http://market.android.com. If you are using an Android 3.0 or newer device, this web site will look very much like an expanded version of the Market that you see on your tablet. This web site was designed to make it very easy to look at the more than 200,000 apps in the Play Store as simply as possible and give you the ability to quickly navigate those apps, install an app on your tablet without even touching it, and write a review of that app, all from the Web.

Figure 5–8. *Play Store from a web browser*

Much like the Store on your tablet, you are greeted first with a large sliding banner of Featured Apps that will slide by you. Beneath the banner you see a larger selection of Featured apps, as well as the apps that have made it to the top of the charts for both Free and Paid apps (as shown in Figure 5–8. As you scroll down this page on your computer, you are given the rest of the apps that fit these categories.

On this page you are also given tabs for Categories and Featured Tablet Apps. Tapping the Categories tab will reveal the same list of categories that is available on your Android Tablet in a scrollable list. The information here is all the same as what you would see on your tablet, just organized a little differently to make it easier to use on your computer.

When you are ready to install an app, things get a little bit different. For users who have both an Android tablet and an Android phone, you will be prompted here to select which device you would like to install the app on (as shown in Figure 5–9). This does not mean you cannot install it on both, but if you are looking to install a tablet optimized Twitter client or a Live Wallpaper for your tablet that you do not want on your phone, you are able to easily make that happen without needing to touch either Android device.

After selecting Buy or Install, depending on the app, you will be asked where you want it to go. The large button at the bottom of this window in Figure 5–9 will reveal a list of devices that are currently logged into with your Google account. Select the device you want, and tap CONTINUE.

Figure 5–9. *Installing an app from the Web Play Store*

The Web Play Store interface is a great way to interact with your devices without actually touching them. As part of what is considered "cloud computing," it is expected that more and more of Google's products will work this way in the future. The tablet, the smartphone, the computer are just acting as windows into the services and activities you want to use. One Google service that already functions this way is Google Books.

Using Play Books

The Play Store isn't just a one-stop shop for all your apps. Google uses the Store as a digital store for its e-books as well. Possessing a massive library of e-books that grows daily, Google offers its e-book reader service, Google Books, to any Android device. As such, any e-book you purchase in the Play Store will be available to read on any Android device, as well as anything with a web browser, such as your PC. On the Play Store home page, there is a Books tab on the top left of the screen right next to Android Apps. Tap that tab, and you'll be taken to the Play Book Store.

> **NOTE:** The Play Book Store for Android tablets is available only on Android 3.0 and newer devices. For Android tablets running a previous version of Android, these books may still be purchased and viewed on your tablet, but you must do so from `http://play.google.com` in a web browser.

The layout of the Play Books tab is nearly identical to that of the Android Apps tab. Here, unlike the Android Apps page, however, everything is themed in blue instead of green, but the navigation is very similar. The Categories view to your right in Figure 5–10 now offers a scrollable list of book genres, from Biographies to Travel. Slide your finger up and down the list to find the genre that interests you, and tap the category to be taken to a list view of those books, where the cover of each book displayed.

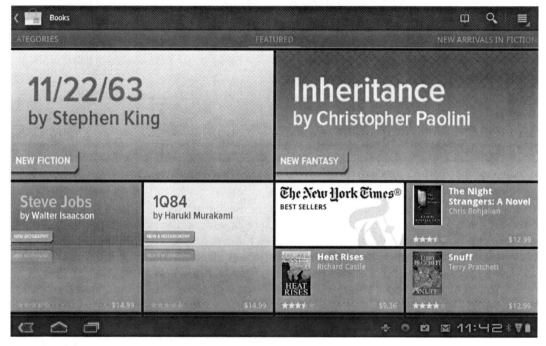

Figure 5–10. *Play Books in the Play Store*

The Snapshot view now shows you popular titles in groups like Top Rated Books, Best Selling Books and Top Free Books. Across the top of the page in Figure 5–10 you are shown featured titles that have been chosen by Google for being New and Noteworthy, a Trending Topic, or a Best Seller. Tapping any of the titles shown on any page will take you to the product page for that book.

Like the Android Apps product page, the Books product page gives you a wealth of information about each title. To the right of the page you are offered a description of the book as given by the author, with reviews about the book underneath that have been written by users who have downloaded the book from the Play Books Store. Underneath reviews you will also find a selection of related titles, with their rating displayed next to the book cover.

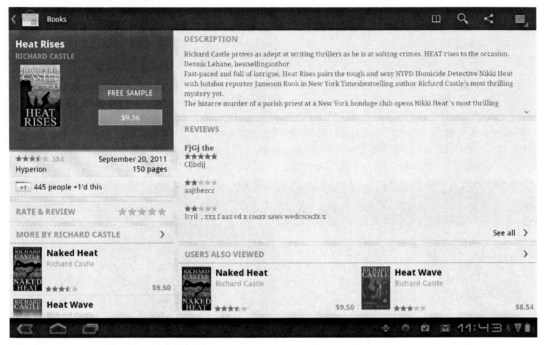

Figure 5–11. *Book View Google Books*

To the right of the product page shown in Figure 5–11 you see the books rating, the cover of the book, and the option to either buy or download the book, depending on whether the book is free. If the book is not free, there is a Free Sample button underneath the Buy button that will give you the first 20 to 25 pages of the book. When you have reached the end of your free sample, Play Books will prompt you to either return to the store's "About this book" product page or allow you to purchase the book, as shown in Figure 5–12.

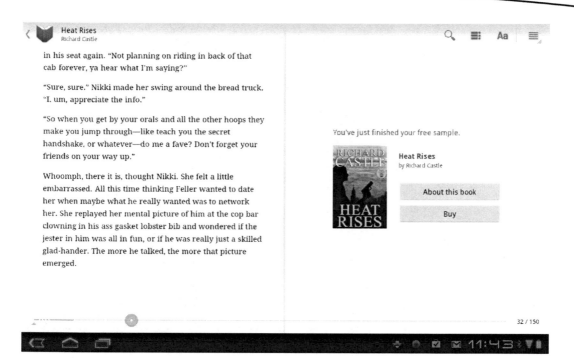

Figure 5–12. *Free Sample end Honeycomb Store for Play Books*

When you choose to purchase a book, you are prompted by the Google Wallet payment gateway to either enter a new credit card or select one that you have saved previously with Google Wallet. Once you have completed your purchase, the book is immediately available in the Google Books app on your tablet, as well as on any web browser.

Using Play Movies

As more and more people have a constant connection to the Internet, the idea of renting your movies from a digital store and not a physical place has become more and more popular. The obvious advantage is that a digital store gives you access to a much larger library, and you never have to worry about whether a copy of the movie you want to watch stories available. With that in mind, Google offers a movie rental service through the Play Store, giving you access to those movies everywhere you are.

Figure 5–13. *Play Movies shop in the Play Store*

From the home screen of the Play Store, locate the Movies tab on the top-right corner and tap the tab. The Movie store, as shown in Figure 5–13, offers a snapshot of the latest movies to be added to the library as soon as you arrive. If you know what movie you are looking for, tap the search icon in the top right of the screen and enter the name of the movie you would like to rent. If you want to browse, swipe your finger from left to right on the screen to reveal the categories that you can browse. Alternatively, if you swipe your finger from right to left on the screen, you will be shown some staff picks, which movies picked out by Google employees as their favorites in the shop. Once you have located a movie you would like to rent, tap the movie title.

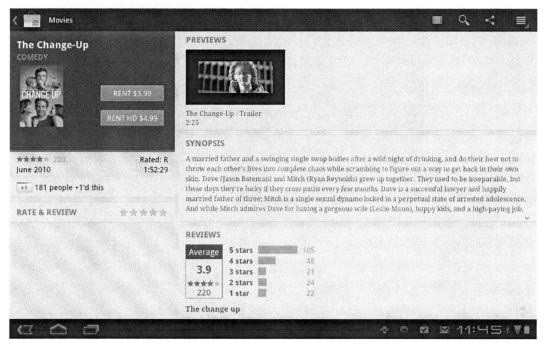

Figure 5–14. *Detailed view of* The Change-Up *found in the Play Movies Store*

As shown in Figure 5–14, when you look at the detailed view of any movie in the shop, you have access to the official trailer for the movie, a synopsis of the file, and reviews of the movie from other people in the Play Store who have seen the movie. Many movies offer you the ability to rent either a standard definition or a high definition version of the film.

> **NOTE:** High-definition versions of videos are much larger than standard definition. If you are viewing a movie over a mobile network, you will use much more of your monthly allowance of data to watch the movie in high definition.

Tap the Rent option you would like, and you will be walked through the checkout process with Google Wallet. When you have completed the checkout process, you will be invited to either download the movie to watch without a connection to the Internet or tap a play button to stream the movie. Additionally, the movie will appear in your Rented movies in the Play Movies app on your Tablet, as shown in Figure 5–15. These movies are not just available on your tablet. Now that you have rented the movie, you can watch it anywhere your Gmail account is connected. If you are at a computer or a GoogleTV, head to YouTube, and the movie will be in the Rented movies section of your account.

Figure 5–15. *Play Movies app with a movie rented from the Play Store*

When you rent a movie, it is available to you for 30 days. You can start watching the movie at any point during that 30-day period. Once you start watching a movie you have rented, you have access to that movie for 24 hours, and then the movie will expire, and you will return the movie.

The Android Market movie shop makes it very easy to grab movies on the go, and because it works so well with the Play Movies app that we will talk more about in Chapter 7, it is a great addition to the Android tablet.

Using Google Play Music

For many people, moving entirely to a digital music provider is impractical. I don't know many people who do not have stacks of CDs, cassette tapes, and even records in their collections. Purchasing all of that music again just to have it digitally available with all of your new music doesn't work out. In Chapter 7, you will learn some of the ways Google makes it easy for you to move music you already own to your tablet, but once you have it there, wouldn't it make more sense to just buy new songs in the same digital format? With the Google Play Music Store in the Play Store, not only can you buy songs, but you can listen to a huge library of free music as well.

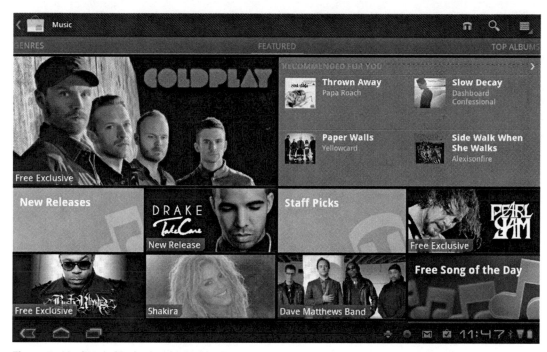

Figure 5–16. *Google Music shop in the Play Store*

Locate the Music tab on the bottom-left corner of the Play Store home screen and tap Music. As shown in Figure 5–16, the Music shop will show you the latest music added to the service as well as some music that has been recommended for you based on your listening history if you use the Google Play Music app. You will also see Google Staff picks on this page.

If you swipe your finger from the left to the right, you will see a list of genres that you can browse to find music you would like to hear. If you swipe from right to left, you will be shown a list of the top selling albums in the Play Store. Additionally, if you know what artist or song you are looking for, you can just tap the search icon in the top-right corner and type what you want to look for. Once you have located an artist, album, or something you would like to hear, you can tap your selection to see the detailed view.

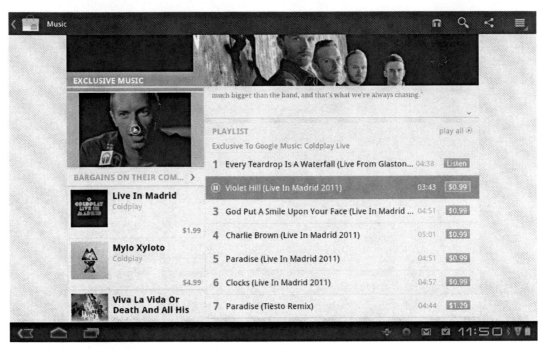

Figure 5–17. *Detailed view of Coldplay in the Google Play Music Store*

The detailed view of an artist in the Google Music shop, as shown in Figure 5–17, will offer you the ability to browse through their albums, listen to songs in the store before you buy, and give you access to any free content they might offer. Some additional content that could be offered with an artist would be interviews or music that is exclusive to the Placy Music Store.

To listen to a song before you buy it, tap the name of the song, and it will start playing immediately if you are connected to the Internet. A pause icon will show up next to the name of the song, giving you the ability to pause and play at will. When you have found a sing or album you like, tap the blue price tag to be taken to Google Wallet.

Once you have completed the purchase, everything you just bought will be immediately available to listen to both on your tablet and in the Google Play Music app.

Summary

The Android Market is a constantly growing and changing ecosystem. As Google adds content types to be sold there, users will become further entangled in using Google as their content provider. Play Apps, Play books, movies, and music...maybe eventually we'll see Google Accessories all sold through this app. The more you use the Store, the more you benefit from having a central location to manage existing apps and services.

In the next chapter, we're going to take a look at using the Camera app on your tablet, as well as apps that interact with the Camera app on your device.

Chapter 6

Using the Camera

It wasn't all that long ago that the idea of a camera on a cell phone was considered crazy. Cameras on phones were widely considered unnecessary, frivolous additions to a device that should just focus on being really good at making phone calls. It took a little while, but having a camera on your phone started to grow in popularity. Once the trend started, it was less than a year before every phone sold had a camera built into it. They weren't great cameras at first, and the screens on most phones were so small and so poor that you would have to transfer the picture to your computer to really enjoy it. That is not the case today.

Today, cameras on mobile devices are expected to take pictures that rival point-and-shoot cameras, as well as record high-quality video to be quickly shared with friends. Now, a new trend has started. Secondary cameras are also being placed facing the user with the same expectations as the other camera. With a front-facing camera, users are able to take pictures of themselves, as well as participate in video calls with other users. This trend, slow starting at first, has quickly spread so that many tablets now have two cameras. In this chapter, we will discuss the different uses for these cameras, including some third-party apps to give you some additional features.

Introducing the Android Camera Apps

Much like the Android phones, the camera on your tablet is controlled using two different apps: the Camera app, which is responsible for taking pictures and recording video, and the Gallery app, which allows you to view the pictures and videos you have taken with your tablet. These apps are not universally identical on every Android tablet, as is the case with Gmail or the Play Store. That's because Google has given Android device manufacturers tools to manipulate the look and feel of the Camera app as they see fit. Most, however, use the app as is. Because of this, all examples in this chapter will be from "stock" Honeycomb.

Let's take a closer look at the two apps, starting with Camera.

Using the Tablet Camera

You can use Android cameras to snap still photos or videos. We'll start by using the camera to shoot single pictures.

To use the Android tablet camera, navigate to the app drawer and select the Camera app from the list. Look for the circular icon with a blue sphere in the middle, identical to the icon on a stock Android phone.

As shown in Figure 6–1, the main screen of the Camera app offers a large viewing area to show you the picture you are about to take. Because most Android tablets are larger than 7 inches, the app has been designed to control everything almost exclusively with your right thumb while you hold the tablet. On the bottom left of the screen, you see a small window with the previous picture taken. Tapping that box will take you into the Gallery app, which we will get into next.

Figure 6–1. *Honeycomb Camera app*

Choosing Camera Settings

The circular dial to the right of the app houses the controls and options for your camera, with a large button at its center used to take a picture. The dial gives you quick access to camera controls:

Flash

Located at the top of the dial, tapping this icon will reveal Flash mode. The three options here are Auto, On, and Off. The app will have Auto set by default the first time you turn the camera on.

White balance

Located to the left of Flash mode on the dial, this button offers you five settings options for the type of light you have around you. These settings include Auto, Incandescent, Daylight, Fluorescent, and Cloudy. Auto is the default option and is set when you use the app for the first time.

Color effect

Located just beneath the white balance setting on the dial, the Color effect has six image filters to choose from. Choosing from Mono, Sepia, Negative, Solarize, Posterize, or None will immediately set the filter on your viewing screen.

Scene mode

Located beneath the Color effect icon on the dial, this button gives you access to a list of preprogrammed settings for various environments. These environments include Action, Portrait, Landscape, Night, Night portrait, Theatre, Beach, and Snow. By default, Auto is set to choose the best settings on the fly.

Camera settings

At the bottom of the dial, you are given a series of settings that control details on how the photo is taken. You can change the store location if your tablet has a microSD, SD, or USB slot. You can adjust the focus mode of the tablet to better suit the type of picture you are taking. You can change the exposure of the image you take, as well as the picture size and picture quality. Many of these settings are for skilled photographers who can get even better pictures from the tablet than with the auto settings.

Zoom

Just above the control dial you'll find large a plus sign (+) and a minus sign (–)that allow you to zoom in and out. Unless your tablet has an optical zoom, you'll be using what is called *digital zoom*. Digital zoom stretches the image to make it look like you are zoomed in on something.

Switching cameras

If your tablet has a front-facing camera, you will see an icon beneath the control dial that allows you to switch quickly from the front to the back camera. Next to this icon is a toggle to switch you from taking a single picture to recording video.

Taking a Photo

After you have set up your camera the way you want, press and hold down on the button in the center of the dial. Once you begin, the camera will focus and alert you that it is ready to take a photo by illuminating an electric green box over the focus area. When you have the shot you want, remove your finger from the button, and the photo will be taken. If you're in a hurry, tapping the camera button quickly will cause the camera to go through the photography steps much faster, but you will often find that pictures will be less clear.

Recording Video

The Camcorder function in the Camera app was designed to be just as simple to use. You still have the same dial to the right, but some of the functions are different. For example, instead of Scene mode, you have Video quality. Video quality allows you to switch between the available modes for your device. These modes will be different based on the type and quality camera you have. The other features, located at the bottom of the dial (as shown in Figure 6–2), are settings for time-lapse video recording. Choose from the time measurements presented when you tap the icon, and you're ready to record. To begin recording, tap the red button in the center of the dial once, and be ready to tap it again when you have finished recording.

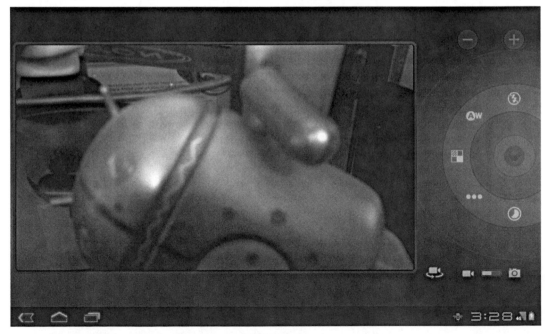

Figure 6–2. *Honeycomb Camcorder function in the Camera app*

Photographing or Recording Yourself

Tablets that have a camera on the front will allow you to easily take photos or record videos of yourself. With tablets that offer a camera in the front as well as the back, there will be a way for you to switch between taking pictures or recording with the rear camera or the front camera.

Look for the camcorder icon to the bottom left of the settings ring, shown in Figure 6–2, that has a rotating arrow underneath it. The camera will, by default, always open with the rear-facing camera in the Camera app. If you are using the camera to video chat, it will default to the front camera. If you tap the icon, it will switch to the opposite camera. When recording video, you can switch the camera as many times as you like, and the app will continue to record from whichever camera is the active camera at the time.

Now that you've taken pictures, shot some video, and played with all of the settings, it's time to go take a look in the Gallery app to see your work!

Using the Gallery

The Gallery app is a central location of all of the images on your tablet. If you download images from the Web, from an e-mail, or even from an app, the pictures will make their way to the Gallery. This app is also where any pictures or video you've taken from your tablet will show up. From inside this app, you can sort through your pictures and video, edit them as you see fit, and share them with the world.

There are two ways to access the Gallery app. You can use the app icon in your app drawer, or you can use the quick access button from inside your Camera app. Either of these buttons will take you to the home screen of the Gallery app.

Grid View

When you first activate the Gallery app, you'll see all of your images and videos are presented in a grid that scrolls to the left and right. Take your finger and drag it across the screen to gain access to more of your pictures and video. If you have collected a large number of pictures or videos, you can sort through them using the controls on the top left of the screen (as shown in Figure 6–3). These filters will drop down when you tap them to allow you to sort by date, time, location, and more. If you'd like to see more information about an image, there is an icon in the top right with an *i* inside. Tap that icon, and tap the image you'd like to see more information about. Once you've found the image or video you want, tap it, and you will be taken to the single-item view.

Figure 6–3. *Honeycomb Gallery app, Grid view*

Single-Item View

The single-item view allows you to see a much larger version of any picture in the grid view, with a few tools so you can get the most out of your photo. If you've found yourself on the wrong image, however, there is a line view at the bottom of this view that allows you to change pictures quickly. Make sure you have the image you want to edit or share.

In the single-item view, you can zoom in an out of the picture by placing two fingers on the screen and moving those two fingers closer together or farther apart. By moving your fingers farther apart, the image will zoom in. By moving your fingers closer together, the image will zoom out. Additionally, if you double tap the screen in a place where you'd like to zoom in automatically, you can do this as well. To return to the original zoom of the picture, simply double tap the center of the screen.

If you'd like to crop an image that you have taken, tap the menu button at the top right of the screen (as shown in Figure 6–4). The list that drops down includes options for rotating the image, setting the image as a contact photo or wallpaper, and cropping the image.

Figure 6–4. *Honeycomb Gallery App, single-item view*

To crop an image, tap the crop function. A box will appear and overlay the image on your screen. Using your fingers, drag the walls of this box to the area you want to crop. Once you've positioned the box where you'd like it to be, select OK from the top right corner, and the image will be cropped. This will create a new image, so don't worry about accidentally destroying a picture.

Now that your picture looks the way you'd like, it is time to share it. The incomplete triangle in the top right of your screen will reveal the different places you can share the photo or video when you tap it. Choose which way you want to share your picture, and you'll be re-directed to that app to share the image or video.

Using Other Apps

Of course, you do not have to use the Camera app that comes with your tablet. In fact, dozens of apps in the Play Store can make your camera do all kinds of new tricks. For example, consider Paper Camera.

As you can see in Figure 6–5, this app is wildly different from the one that Google gives you. This app gives you a new set of filters and features to play with, allowing you to have some fun with your camera that isn't possible with the native app. Once you've taken a picture, the app deposits the image right in your Gallery to edit and share, just like the Camera app.

Figure 6–5. *Paper Camera app*

Taking photos is fun, but what if you'd like to do more with editing those photos on your tablet? The Play Store has plenty of options for you as well. Adobe has a version of their popular photo-editing software on Android tablets called Adobe Photoshop Express.

Adobe's free app allows you to edit and change any photo in your Gallery with many more tools than what is included in the Gallery (as shown in Figure 6–6). Once you have made edits, the app will save the picture as though it were a new image, allowing you to keep the picture you originally took.

Figure 6–6. *Adobe Photoshop Express app.*

Summary

Although you are less likely to pull out your big tablet to snap a photo, especially if you have a real camera or a phone, the camera is still a powerful tool on any tablet, and the Play Store is full of ways to make using the camera more fun and more productive.

In the next chapter, you will learn how to turn your tablet into the center of your digital entertainment world with music, movie, and games on your tablet.

Chapter 7

Music, Movies, and Games

Your Android tablet is not just a web-connected device for productivity and e-mail. It's also a portal for nearly every form of digital entertainment out there. If you own a CD, if you ever bought a movie with a digital copy, or even if you have a Netflix subscription, your tablet can be used to store, stream, and enjoy movies anywhere you are.

In this chapter, you will learn how to put music and movies on your tablet and how to stream that content from an online service to your tablet. We won't stop at music and movies either, because your Android tablet also has access to a multiple libraries of games of all kinds. You will learn about the many different things you can do with games on your tablet and some accessories you can use to turn your tablet into a complete entertainment system.

Listening to Music on Your Tablet

You probably own a shelf full of CDs. You might have copied some of those CDs onto your computer. You might even be using a music manager like iTunes or Windows Media Player for your collection of music. If you said "That's me" to any of those things, then you will be able to move your music to your Android tablet pretty simply.

Maybe you don't have a collection of music on your computer, though. Maybe you use Internet radio or some other form of Internet-based service for your music. Your Android tablet supports you as well. Essentially, any current way of consuming music can be enhanced by your Android tablet. To make it easy, we're going to break down the steps for moving music to your tablet.

Playing Stored Music

Whether you own a stack of CDs or you've been downloading music forever, your Android tablet is designed to make it easy to move your music from your computer to your tablet.

> **NOTE:** To connect your Android tablet to your computer, you will need a USB cable, preferably the cable that came with your device.

Connect your tablet to your computer. Once the tablet and the computer detect the connection, you will see a pop-up on your desktop and a notification on your tablet (as shown in Figure 7–1).

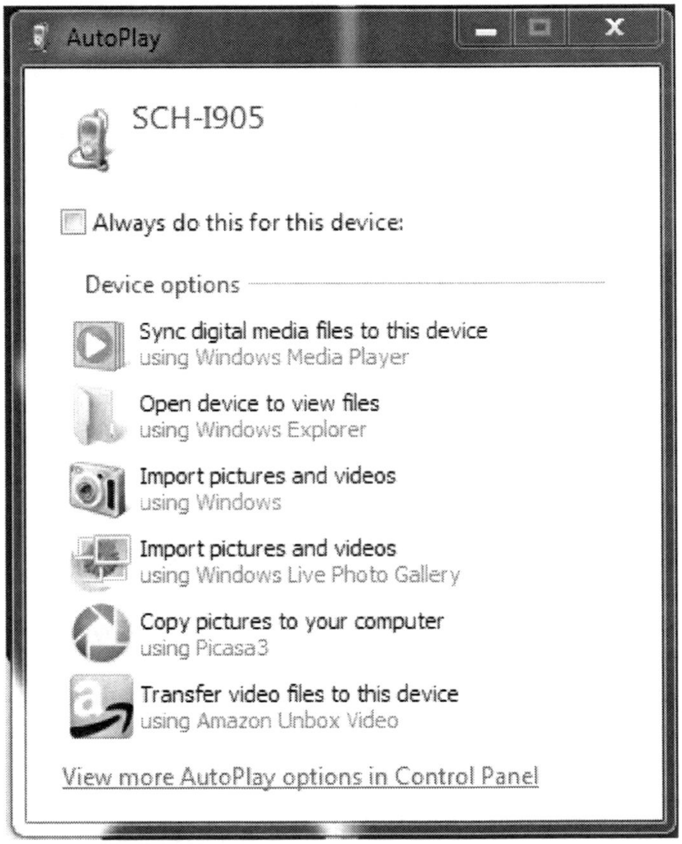

Figure 7–1. *Windows 7 detecting your tablet*

Once you have the folder open, double-click the Music folder. Once you are inside your Music folder, you will need to locate the music on your computer. All you need to do is move the music from your existing music folder to the Music folder on the tablet. To do this, drag your music from your music folder to the Music folder on your tablet (as shown in Figure 7–2).

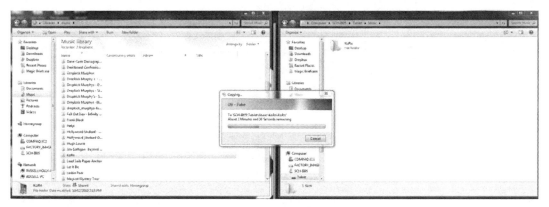

Figure 7–2. *Transferring music from your computer to your tablet*

Once you have dragged music to your tablet's music folder, a pop-up progress bar will show you how long it will take for the music to transfer to your tablet, as shown in Figure 7–2.

> **WARNING:** Do not disconnect your tablet from your computer during a transfer. If the tablet becomes disconnected during this process, you will risk the music not transferring or becoming unplayable, and you will need to restart this process.

When the music has finished transferring, you will be able to disconnect your tablet by removing the USB cable and are now ready to begin listening to music on your tablet.

Locate the Google Play Music app in your app drawer and tap once to open it. Every time you open the Music app, it will search your tablet for new music to play, so the songs you just transferred to the tablet will already be in the app, ready to play.

The Carousel view for the Music app allows you to drag your finger across the screen and be presented with the album art for all of the songs that you have transferred to your tablet (shown in Figure 7–3). In this view, you can select a specific album and display its tracks by tapping the album art.

Figure 7–3. *Google Play Music's Carousel view*

In Album view, you are shown all of the songs within an album (as shown in Figure 7–4). Tapping any song in the list will play it. The controls you need to play, stop, pause, and adjust the volume of your songs are always available at the bottom of the screen.

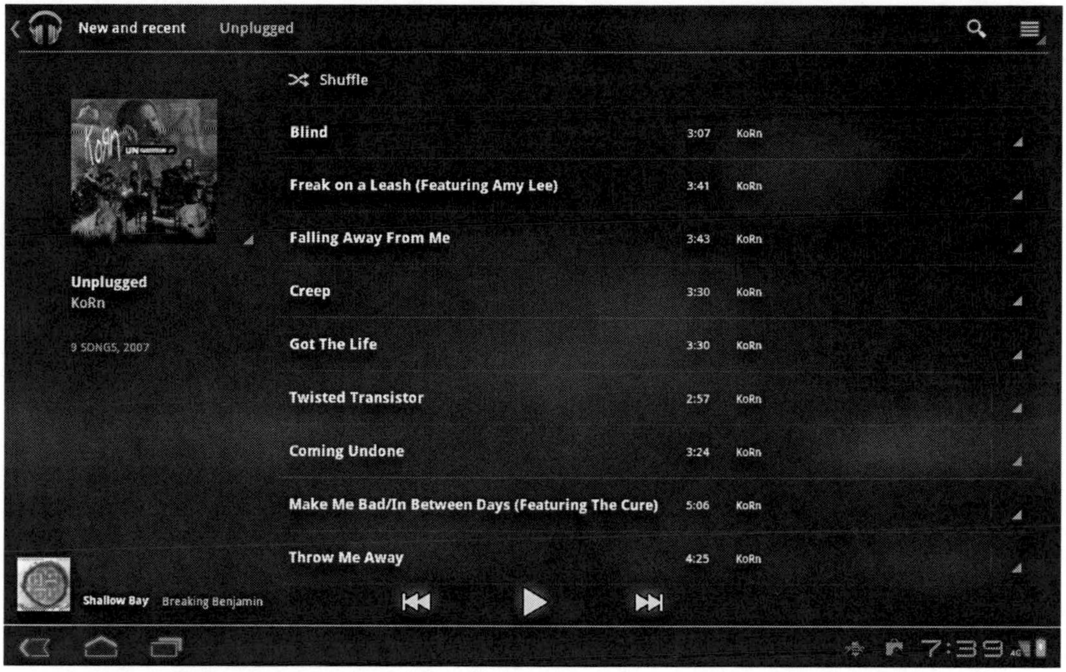

Figure 7–4. *Google Play Music's list view*

You can organize the songs inside the Google Play Music app in any way you choose. If you tap the words next to the headphones icon at the top left of the app, you will be presented with a list of ways you can display your music titles. For example, if you select the Songs view, you will be presented with a list of all of the songs in your inventory (see Figure 7–5. This way, if you choose the Shuffle option at the top of the list, the Google Play Music app will shuffle through all of the songs you have.

Figure 7–5. *Google Play Music's sorting menu*

Once your music is playing, you can leave the app and go use other apps on your tablet. Your music will continue to play. Select a song you want to hear, and tap the home button to be taken to your home screen (as shown in Figure 7–6).

From any point on your tablet, you can select the digital clock at the bottom-right corner of the home screen to bring up your settings and notifications quick panel (as shown in Figure 7–6). If you have music playing, basic music controls will be displayed in this panel, allowing you to quickly pause, play, or skip tracks in your Google Play Music app without leaving what you are doing.

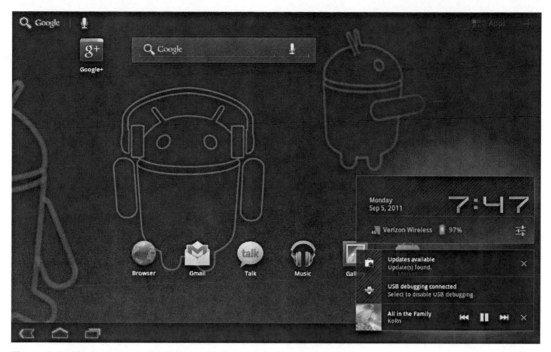

Figure 7–6. *Music player on the Honeycomb home screen*

Using Other Music Apps

So, maybe you have a pretty extensive library and you really don't want to keep your tablet plugged into your computer for so long. There's a solution to that, but it requires an app or two that doesn't come standard with your tablet.

Head to the Play Store and grab the doubleTwist app and the doubleTwist AirSync app. doubleTwist is an alternative to the Google Play Music app that comes with your tablet. Once you've installed doubleTwist, you will be prompted to allow it to e-mail you the application for your computer. Enter your e-mail address in the app, and then head over to your computer and install the program.

> **NOTE:** For this to work, your computer and your tablet need to be on the same network. You will need a Wi-Fi connection for your tablet to connect to.

Once you have the program installed on your computer, tap the AirSync button in the doubleTwist app. This icon will be at the bottom left of the app. Once you've done this, the app will begin to walk you through the process of connecting your tablet to your computer via Wi-Fi (as shown in Figure 7–7).

Figure 7–7. *doubleTwist Honeycomb app setup*

This process begins with doubleTwist providing you with a five-digit code. On your computer, locate and select your username from the panel on the left side of the doubleTwist app. This username will have the AirSync icon next to it.

When you select your username, you will be asked to enter the five-digit code that was just provided to you by the doubleTwist app on the tablet (as shown in Figure 7–8). As long as you correctly copied this information over, your tablet and your computer will immediately let you know you have succeeded.

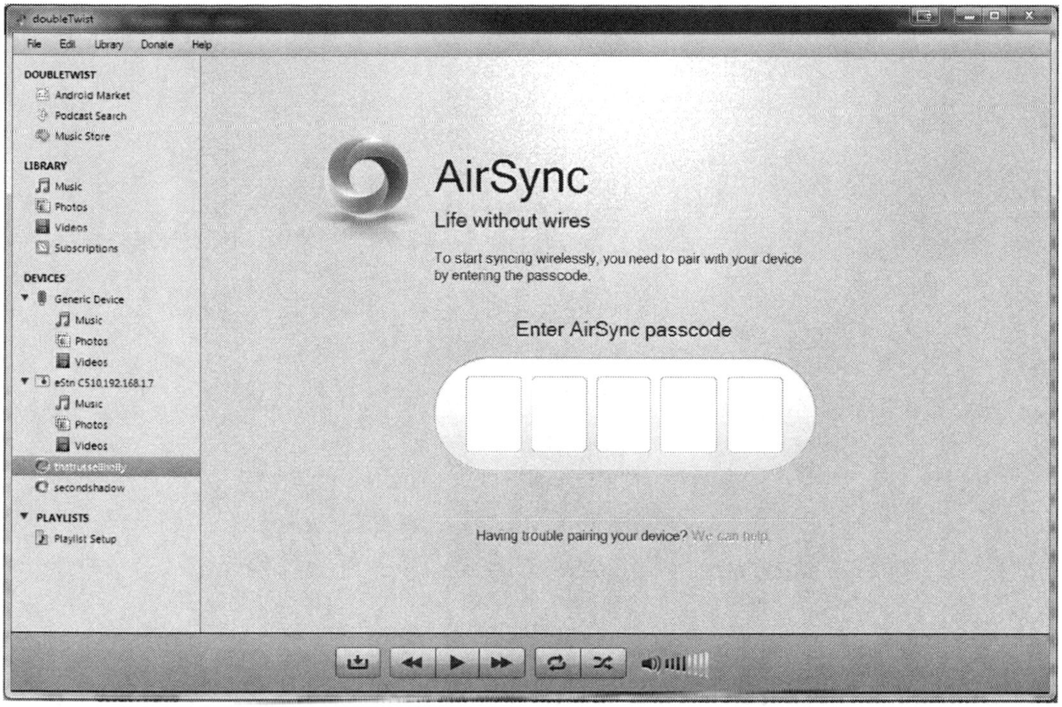

Figure 7–8. *DoubleTwist AirSync PC setup*

When your tablet gives you the success screen shown in Figure 7–9, you will be able to transfer your music to your tablet without connecting it to a computer. From the computer, select the Music tab and make sure the "Sync music to my device" box is checked. You will then see the orange Sync button light up in the bottom-right corner of the program (see Figure 7–10). When you click that icon, your music will begin to transfer to your tablet. While this is happening, you will see the AirSync icon in your notification tray on your tablet. It is important that your tablet stay on the Wi-Fi connection until the transfer has finished.

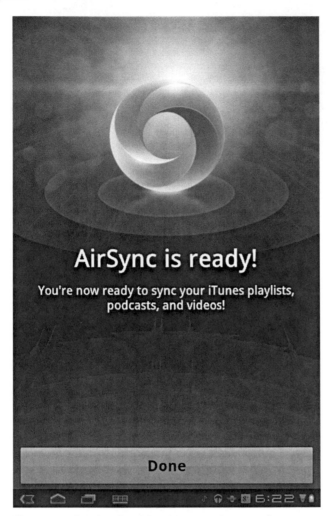

Figure 7–9. *DoubleTwist AirSync Honeycomb app confirm screen*

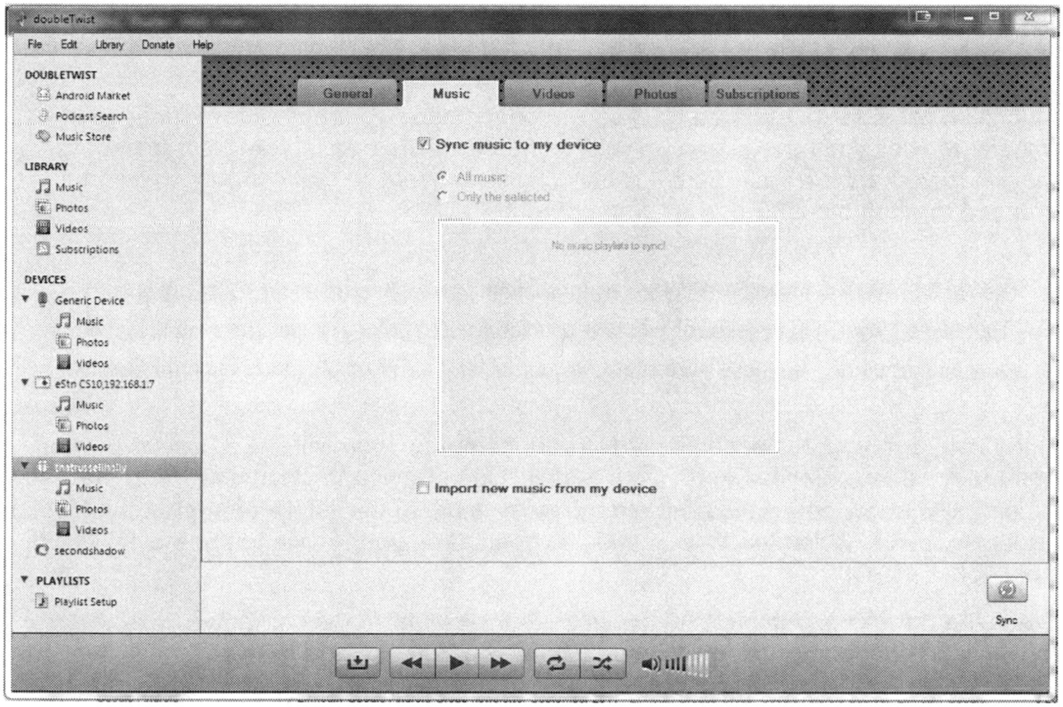

Figure 7-10. *DoubleTwist AirSync music page*

There are many other ways to enjoy music in the Play Store, and you should feel empowered to install as many different music apps as you want and explore how the features provided by those apps benefit you the best.

Slacker Radio, for example, offers you the ability to create a personalized radio station that will play music only from artists of your choosing. Or, if you find yourself in that painful situation where the name of a song is on the tip of your tongue but you just can't name it, try the SoundHound app. You can play part of a song or even just sing to the app, and it will tell you the name of the artist and the track you are listening to.

Being able to bring your music with you wherever you go is a great way to not only have your entire library at your fingertips but also have a backup in case anything happens to a CD or your home computer. As great as it is to do this with music, you may be surprised to find you can do the same thing with movies.

Watching Movies on Your Tablet

Many movies contain an additional digital copy when released to DVD today. This service is provided for those who would prefer to watch their movies on their computer, smartphone, MP4 player, or tablet. Many of those devices, especially tablets, don't have a DVD player built in, so a digital copy is needed. Additionally, there are a number of movie-streaming services that provide you with the ability to watch a movie over the Internet, without it being stored on your computer.

Watching Stored Movies on Your Tablet

Much like we did with music, a USB cable connected to your computer is needed to transfer movies you have stored on your computer to your tablet. Before transferring movies to your tablet, make sure it is fully charged, because many tablets cannot be charged through the USB port on your computer.

> **NOTE:** The average standard-definition feature-length movie takes up about 700MB of space. That same movie in high definition can take up as much as 2GB of storage. This means that not only do movies take up much more space on your tablet, they also take much longer to transfer.

Once you have your tablet connected to your computer, you will see a pop-up on your computer asking you what to do next. Select "Open Device to view Files" from that list. When the window opens, you will see a Movies folder in the list. Double-click the Movies folder to open it. When the Movies folder is open, drag your movie to the Movies folder from your computer.

When the transfer is complete, disconnect your tablet from the computer. Now that the movie is on your computer, go to your Videos app from the app drawer.

The Videos app on your tablet has two modes, one for showing streaming videos and one for stored videos. Select the Personal Videos tab from that top left of the app, as shown in Figure 7–11. The view will change to a horizontal list of available videos to watch, including videos you have transferred to the tablet or purchased directly over the Internet from an online store. This list will also include videos that you have recorded with your tablet, should it have a camera on it. Tap the movie you want to watch, and the movie will fill the screen. To exit the app, tap the home button or the back button to go back to the menu.

Figure 7-11. *Personal Videos tab of Honeycomb Videos app*

Watching Streamed Movies on Your Tablet

Should you rent movies online one at a time or pay a monthly subscription to access a library of movies? These options have been available for PCs and phones for quite some time, and now they're available on tablets as well, making it possible for you to access your account with those movie services wherever you have an Internet connection. For movie rentals, Google includes its own service, Google Videos, on your tablet. For subscription services, we'll cover several of the options available to you in the Play Store.

Renting Google Play Movies

Google Play Movies app for Android allows you to rent movies from its library and then watch them anywhere you are connected to the Internet. You can watch your rentals on your PC, your tablet, your Google TV, or your smartphone, and you can switch back and forth between these devices, and the movie you have rented will pick up where it left off. Movies you rent are available to you for 30 days until you start watching it, and then they are available to you for 24 hours.

From your app drawer, tap the Google Play Movies app. When the app loads, you are presented with the list of top-rented videos across the bottom, with your active rentals in the middle of the app (see Figure 7–12). Since this is your first time using the app, you have no rentals, so let's go get one. Tap the Shop icon in the top right of the screen.

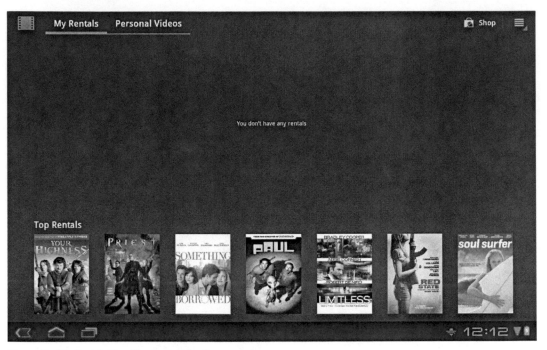

Figure 7–12. *Google Play Movies app for Honeycomb*

The Google Videos shop is part of the Play Store, so there is no need to register a new account. Your Google profile is automatically recognized, and if you have already purchased an app or a book, your Google checkout information is there as well. As you browse the categories for movies, note that the price for each movie is next to the movie cover and title (as shown in Figure 7–13). Tap the movie you want to watch to see a detailed view of the movie.

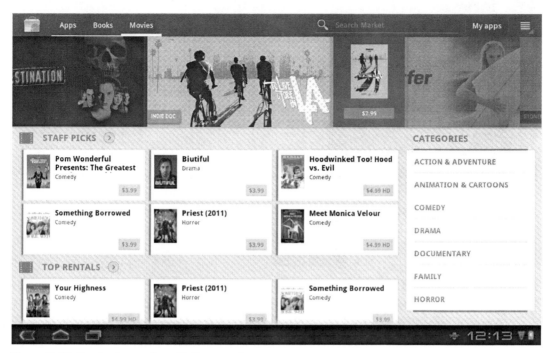

Figure 7–13. *Purchasing movies with Honeycomb app*

The detailed view shows you a synopsis of the film, followed by a preview of the film (see Figure 7–14). Scroll down with your fingers to show additional information about the cast and credits. From this page, you can share details about the movie using the Share button in the top right, or you can browse related films if you haven't found exactly what you are looking for. To purchase the movie, you can choose between standard definition and HD; just tap your choice and complete the purchase through Google Wallet.

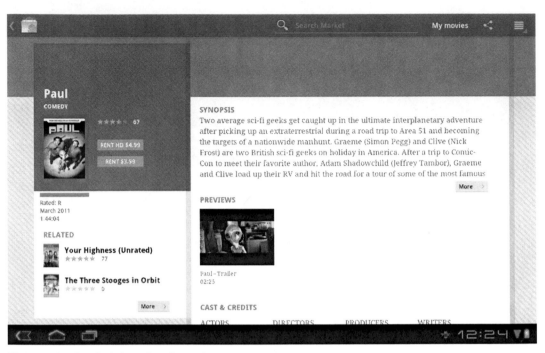

Figure 7-14. *Detailed view of movie purchase*

> **WARNING:** High-definition videos are much larger than standard definition. If you are watching movies over a mobile data connection, you will be consuming your monthly allotment of data much faster with an HD movie.

Once the purchase is complete, the video will show up immediately in your My Rentals section of the Google Play Movies app (as shown in Figure 7–15). To watch the movie, tap the art for it, and you will be taken to the movie. Now that the movie is in the app, it will also appear on YouTube on any computer you have logged in to.

Figure 7–15. *Play Movies app with purchased movie*

Viewing Hulu, Netflix, Blockbuster Videos, and More

Many web-based video services have Android apps as well, allowing you to access that content from your tablet so long as you have an Internet connection. Search the Play Store for your service of choice, and install the app just like you would any other. If you have an account with any of these services, you will be prompted to log in (see the Netflix login screen shown in Figure 7–16).

Figure 7–16. *Netflix app on Honeycomb*

If you have never used these services before, you will be prompted to create an account. If the service you are interested in has a monthly fee like Netflix and Hulu or a per-video fee like Blockbuster, you will be asked to store your payment information with their service, not through Google Wallet.

Viewing Tablet Videos on Your TV

If you're set up with any of the video-watching solutions we've discussed, you've created a pretty powerful way to bring video with you anywhere. When traveling, visiting with friends and family, or even just providing some entertainment for the kids on the road, video can be a great distraction. Chances are, however, that your tablet isn't the biggest screen in your house. If your tablet has an HDMI port, you can connect your tablet to your TV with an HDMI cable and watch all of your video on the TV instead. If you're not sure whether your tablet has an HDMI port, be sure to check Chapter 1.

Another way your tablet can connect to your TV is through wireless services. Many new HDTVs support a technology called DLNA. This technology allows you to wirelessly stream videos stored on your tablet to your HDTV. There are many DLNA-ready TVs, and several apps in the Play Store offer step-by-step instructions. You will not be able to use DLNA to show things like Hulu or Netflix on your TV, but any video you have stored on your tablet will play.

There are more and more things that you can do with your tablet every day when it comes to video. That tiny computer can become your entertainment center, your babysitter, or your travel companion all with the right app.

Playing Games on Your Tablet

My first mobile phone had a game on it called Snakes. My phone had a 2-inch screen with a blue backlight that kind of hurt my eyes if I stared at it for too long, much less tried to read a whole lot on it. Still, I remember Snakes being my go-to thing whenever I was waiting in line for something, when I was stopped at a red light, or even when I just couldn't get to sleep. The game wasn't anything special. It didn't have the intense graphics of a PC game or offer the comfortable controller of a console game or the novelty of a handheld gaming system. The game was just there when I wanted something to do, so I played it.

Fast-forward to today, when mobile games like Angry Birds have become household names. The mobile gaming environment has become its own platform. Game designers no longer see making a game for a phone as something extra but instead see it as mandatory.

Now, we have tablets. Bigger screens, more powerful hardware, and much greater capacity for battery life all mean the games you will have access to will be rich, engaging, and potentially capable of consuming your attention for hours at a time.

Finding Games

Games on an Android work just like any other app, and they are available from several sources. We'll look at two: Play Store and Nvidia Tegra Zone.

Finding Play Store Games

If you head to the Play Store on your tablet or to http://play.google.com on your computer's web browser, you will see a Games section on the home page of the Play Store.

Games are organized in the Play Store like any other type of app. Search the categories for a game you might like, and install it like you would any other app (as shown in Figure 7–17). Some games are much larger than others and will take up a lot more space on your tablet. Be sure to check the size of the game in the detailed view of the app in the Store.

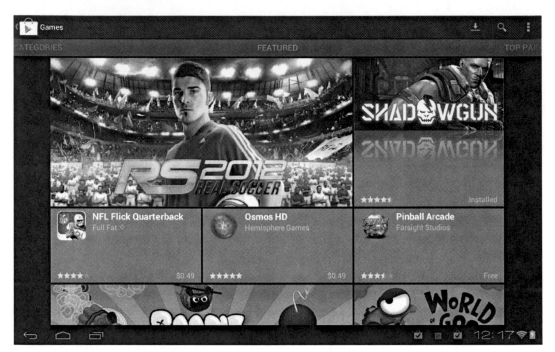

Figure 7–17. *Games view of Play Store*

Finding Nvidia Tegra Zone Games

Google's Play Store comes preinstalled and offers a wide variety of games of all types. For some tablets, however, certain high-quality games are designed specifically for tablets that include their special processors. Such is the case with the Nvidia Tegra Zone. If your Android tablet runs on the Nvidia Tegra 2 processor, you are able to use the games found in the Tegra Zone.

The Tegra Zone suite of games delivers a visual experience comparable to some games found on traditional game consoles. In fact, if you have an HDMI-compatible system, you can even connect your tablet to the TV and play Tegra Zone games on the TV, just like you would a console.

If you locate a game in the Tegra Zone you would like to purchase or install, you can tap the green Get It Now button and will be taken to a checkout screen in the Play Store that allows you to purchase the apps the same way you would inside the Play Store (as shown in Figure 7–18). Games purchased from the Tegra Zone will update just like every other app you install from the Play Store.

Figure 7–18. *Tegra Zone on Honeycomb*

Adding a Controller

Your Android tablet has a pretty big screen. Because of this, it's not always easy to put your hands in the right places to play some of the more action-oriented games. Being able to move your car by turning your tablet to the left or to the right is cool, but sometimes that traditional console style controller is really the most comfortable device to use. Honeycomb tablets support the ability to connect a USB controller to your tablet (like the one shown in Figure 7–19) and play your game with the accuracy and stability of a traditional controller.

Figure 7–19. *Controller connected to Honeycomb tablet*

Summary

When it comes to entertainment, your Android tablet is capable of delivering just about every kind of experience you can imagine and many that probably haven't even crossed your mind yet. Whether it's a calm game like Scrabble, the latest blockbuster movie, or a recording of your favorite band, you can view and play it on your tablet.

In the next chapter, you will learn some best practices in taking your Android tablet with you everywhere you go and using it to your benefit.

Chapter 8

Using Your Android Tablet Wherever You Go

So far in this book, you have learned how to make your tablet be the center of your Google experience, as well as how to have some fun with it. Your Android tablet can replace many of the functions that you would normally have to sit in front of a computer to do: managing e-mail, surfing the Web, video chatting, and much more. But, your tablet is capable of doing much more for you. In fact, many users are replacing their laptops with tablets when they are on the go, because they are so portable.

In this chapter, you will learn how your tablet can extend your desktop, as well as provide new tools that you can use to explore the world around you.

Making Your Tablet More Like Your Desktop

More and more things are done on our computers every day. Fewer people open the Yellow Pages than go to www.YellowPages.com to look for an address or phone number anymore. Google's search engine is one of most used web sites on the planet for this very reason. Using your computer is great for getting information quickly, but unless you decide to print that information or write it down, it stays on your computer. If you have an Android tablet, there's a quick and easy way to accomplish the same goals without printing or writing.

Alternatively, say you need access to documents on the go. You could e-mail the files back and forth to yourself or walk around with a flash drive in your pocket, but if you have a tablet, there are tools at your disposal to be smarter about how you handle those documents. In this section, we'll look at tools for syncing your tablet with other Google apps and for storing documents where they can be reached from any device.

Sync Your Tablet with Google Chrome

If you use the Web a lot, chances are good your web browser has saved a few things for you. You probably have a couple of bookmarks for your favorite sites, or maybe when you order something off the Internet, your address is already saved on the web site. Maybe when you log in to Facebook, you find that you are already logged in because your browser has saved your spot. These are all really nice features to have, but they go away immediately when you move to a new device, since nothing is saved. If you use Google Chrome with an Android tablet, this is not the case at all.

Open Google Chrome, like we did in Figure 8–1, and click the wrench icon to the far right of your toolbar. Head to the bottom of the list that just popped up and select Settings. The Options tab will open in Chrome, showing you all of the things you can change in Chrome. Select Personal Stuff from the left and select SYNC, the first option to appear on the new page.

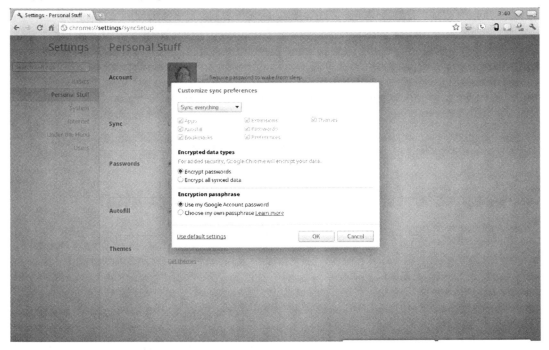

Figure 8–1. *Chrome Sync setup form on a computer*

Once you have enabled syncing from your web browser, you will be able to activate it on your tablet and begin transferring information. From your home screen, tap the clock in the bottom-right corner and select the Settings icon from the pop-up. Find Accounts & Sync in the list and tap it, revealing the option to select an account. Tap your account to continue to the options for your account, and select "Sync browser" from the list.

Within a couple of minutes your bookmarks, your passwords, and any autofill fields you might have saved will be synced to your tablet browser, giving you the ease of use you already have on your computer.

Sync Your Tablet with Your Phone

Being able to sync everything that you already have on your computer is a valuable tool, but what happens when you are in the middle of reading an article on your favorite news web site and you have to run out the door? What happens when you've looked up a direction on Google Maps and you want to move it to your tablet? Google's answer to this is Chrome to Phone, a service that allows you to send information from the web browser on your computer to your tablet.

The first thing you will need to do is install Chrome to Phone on your computer. You start by heading to Google.com and searching for *Chrome to Phone*. The first option you will see listed is a Chrome to Phone Extension link. Click this link to be taken to the installation page. From here you will see a blue box like the one in Figure 8–2 with an Install button in the bottom right. Click Install, and in seconds you will have a small phone icon with a yellow arrow in the top right of your browser, next to the wrench.

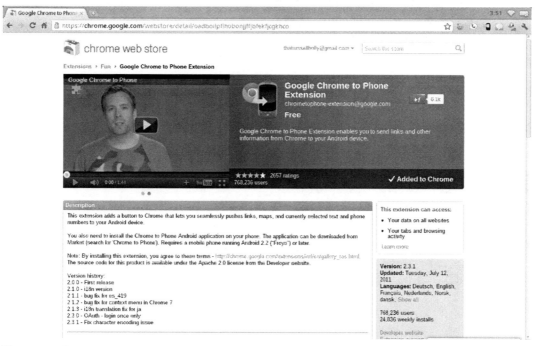

Figure 8–2. *Chrome to Phone install screen in Google Chrome for PC*

Click this icon, and you will be prompted to choose a Gmail address to log in with. Enter the e-mail address you used on your Android tablet. Once this is complete, you will be finished with the browser and be ready to move to your tablet.

From your home screen, head to your app drawer, and go to the Play Store. Once there, tap the Search button and search for *Chrome to Phone*. The first option to appear will be the Google-made app that complements the extension you just installed, as shown in Figure 8–3. Select Install on the free app, and open the app once the installation has finished. When you load the app, Chrome to Phone will ask you to verify which Gmail account you want to sync with. Make sure you select the same account you entered for the Chrome extension. Once this is completed, you will be prompted to allow the app to access your Gmail account. Select Accept from the options, and you will be presented with the option shown in Figure 8–4 either to automatically launch links that are sent to the phone or to launch the links only when prompted to do so.

Figure 8–3. *Google Chrome to Phone install screen from the Play Store for tablets*

This option is entirely your preference. If you choose to automatically launch links, when you click the Chrome to Phone button on your desktop, the data web site you have sent to your tablet will pop up immediately. If you select "Let me launch links manually," you will be given a pop-up so you can choose whenever you aren't busy to launch it on your tablet.

Figure 8–4. *Google Chrome to Phone setup on tablet*

Now that you have everything set up, you are ready to use Chrome to Phone whenever you like. Any time you are on a web site you would like to send to your phone, just click the Chrome to Phone button in the top right of your browser window on your computer, and no matter where your tablet is, the web site will be sent to your device. If you have chosen to manually accept the links, you will be given a notification in the bottom right of your screen, as shown in Figure 8–5. If you are using Google Maps on your computer at http://maps.google.com and select the Chrome to Phone button, the Google Maps application will open on your tablet instead of just the web site.

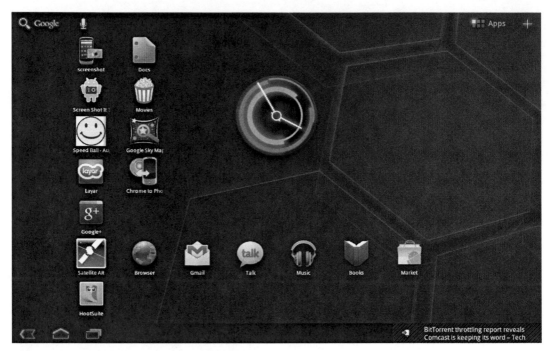

Figure 8–5. *Google Chrome to Phone notification*

Store Files in the Cloud with Dropbox

Google doesn't offer its own cloud-based storage system, but the Play Store has several options at your disposal to make accessing files on your tablet quick and easy. The example we will use for this book will be Dropbox. Dropbox provides a service that allows users to store files online but access them from anywhere with the app or from a web page. Every account gets 2GB of online storage for free, offering more storage for paid accounts. To create an account, go to www.dropbox.com on your computer.

From the Dropbox web site, shown in Figure 8–6, select the Download Dropbox button and install the application. Part of this installation will be to create a local folder. The files you put in this folder will be automatically uploaded to the Dropbox service. Place any documents, spreadsheets, or files of any kind there.

Figure 8-6. *Dropbox.com download page on a computer*

Now that you have files to see, go to the Play Store on your Android tablet and search for *Dropbox*. Dropbox is a free app, so just tap Install to download the app. Once the app has downloaded, tap Open.

The Dropbox app will ask you either to log in to an existing account or to create a new one. If you followed the previous instructions, you should be able to select "login to existing account." Enter your username and password and log in to the application. This will need to be done only once.

Now that you are logged into the app, you will see the files you have uploaded to Dropbox, as shown in Figure 8–7. Most files can be viewed just by tapping any of the files. To edit a file, you will need to press and hold a specific file. This will pop up a menu that includes an option to download a file. When you have downloaded the file, you will be able to edit the file on your tablet using whatever app you choose.

Figure 8–7. *Dropbox app for tablets, list view*

Augmenting Your Reality

The Internet is full of information. You can look up movie show times, search for a restaurant close to the theater, and even get a review of the restaurant's quality. Or, maybe you are sightseeing in a place you have never been and you'd like to do a tour without a tour guide. The technology in your tablet, coupled with a kind of software called *augmented reality*, offers you a whole new way to complete tasks. This technology takes the view of the world as we see it and overlays computer-generated information on top of that view so you can see the information and the real world at the same time.

Navigate the Night Sky with Google Sky Map

One of the easiest ways to understand augmented reality is to take a look at Google Sky Map. Head to the Play Store and search for *Google Sky Map*. This is a free app, so just click Install. When the app has finished installing, select Open.

The first thing you will notice about Google Sky Map, shown in Figure 8–8, is that you are now looking at a map of stars in the sky. That's mostly true; what you are actually looking at is a map of the stars in the sky behind your tablet. As you move your tablet around, the map will change to show you stars in relation to the location of the tablet. You can move your tablet all around you and see the night sky. This app also allows you to search for specific stars, planets, and more.

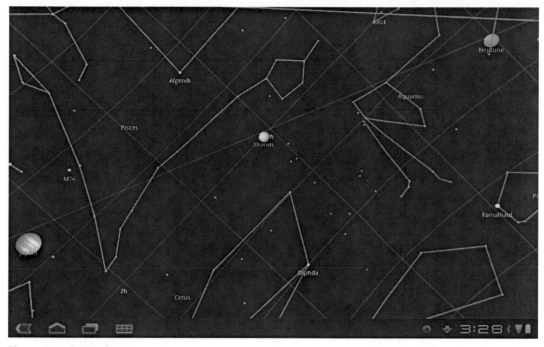

Figure 8–8. *Google Sky Map*

Tap the Menu button on the bottom-left corner of the screen. Among the options that will pop up, you will see the Search button. When the Search field pops up, enter the name of any celestial object you would want to find and press Enter. The app will create a ring like the one in Figure 8–9 that will guide you to the actual location of the solar object in relation to your device. When you get to the object you are looking for, the ring will turn orange. This app is great for anybody looking to play with the stars.

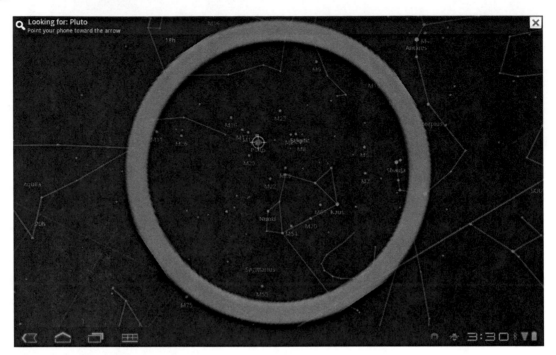

Figure 8–9. *Google Sky Map Search view*

Learn More About a Location with Layar

Augmented reality is a cool concept, but it becomes truly useful only when real-world data is given to the software to help you out. A perfect example of such an app is Layar. Unlike many other augmented reality apps, Layar allows you to take multiple data sets and place them on your screen in layers. Head to the Play Store and search for *Layar*. This is a free app, so just click Install. When the app has finished installing, select Open.

From the start, as shown in Figure 8–10, you will be able to choose from many different kinds of layers. From the menu, tap Popular and look at the list of the most popular sources. From this menu, select Yelp from the list. Yelp is a service that collects all kinds of data on restaurants, shopping, and entertainment. The service also allows for users to rate their experience with a local business and offer reviews. Tap the Launch button in the top right of the app to begin this layer.

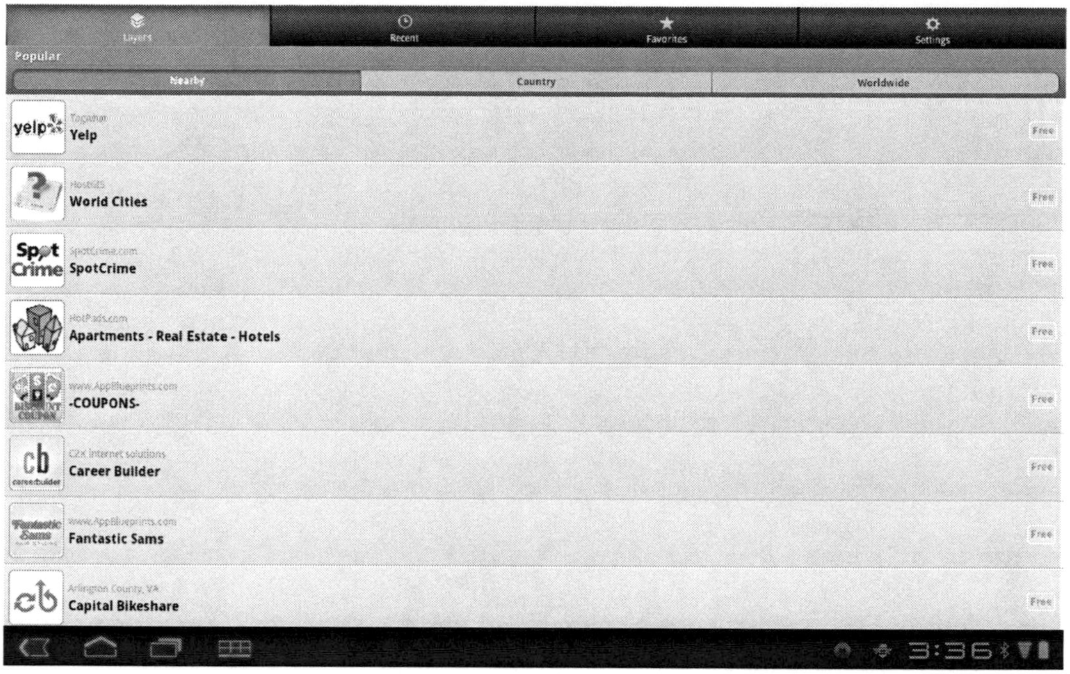

Figure 8–10. *Layar Popular layers view*

The first thing you will notice is that you are now looking through the camera on your tablet, as though you were about to take a picture. You will also see a grid fall into place with colored triangles, just like what you see in Figure 8–11. Each of these triangles is a location that has been found by Yelp. If you tap any of the locations, you will be given more information about the location. The locations on the map have been placed in their geographical location, so if you see a location on your screen, it is literally in the direction your tablet is currently pointing. If you need more specific directions, tap the icon and choose "Take me there" from the menu that pops up, and you will be taken to Google Maps for navigation to that location.

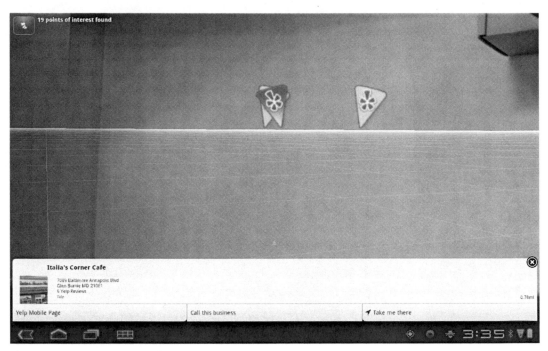

Figure 8–11. *Layar Yelp layer view*

Layar has many more uses than just finding a restaurant or a movie theater. You can look for historical locations with Wikipedia, search for apartments for rent with HotPads, or even have some fun with the Dragon Catcher layer. All of these options use the power of your location and your camera to turn your tablet into a heads-up display for your whole world.

Summary

Your tablet can offer you the ability to extend your home computer wherever you are. There are more apps every day that offer even more of these critical tools that can make it possible to bring your tablet closer and closer to being a computer replacement.

As you begin to move around more with your tablet, you will slowly realize that you can do a lot more with it comfortably. While it is certainly great for music and movies, you can also view PDF files, edit documents and spreadsheets, and even take video files and make a movie. Storing all of that stuff on your tablet can take up a lot of room, and moving the files from your computer to your tablet means getting your USB cable out and sitting and waiting. Fortunately, there's no need for that with cloud storage, and there are several options available to you in Chapter 10 that work on both your computer and your tablet to share files without storing them on your tablet.

In the next chapter, you will learn how to use your tablet not just as a great tool for at home and while you are out and about but also to get more done in the workplace with your Android tablet.

Chapter 9

Using Your Tablet at Work

So far, we've covered a lot of information when it comes to using your Android tablet in your personal life. For many people, however, it is difficult to mix personal devices and work devices. Your employer will have concerns, and even if you run your own business, you'll want to take steps to protect its assets.

For any system administrator, there are concerns when it comes to the security of adding a tablet device to a corporate network, such as the sensitivity of information being shared with the device and what to do when an employee leaves the company. For businesses, certain tools make bringing your Android tablet into the workplace much easier to deal with. We'll show you how in this chapter.

Securing Your Tablet

The best way to convince your employer or client that it's OK to store proprietary information on your Android tablet is by proving that it is a secure device. Fortunately, this is made easy in just a few steps on your Android tablet. In this section, you will learn how to secure your tablet by locking the screen, encrypting the information you store there, making it easy to identify you as the owner in case it's lost (or stolen), and installing and managing the secure credentials you need to access your workplace systems.

Locking Your Screen

Right now, when you want to get into your tablet, all you have to do is slide the bubble to the ring and the device unlocks. This is convenient, but it also means that anybody can pick up your tablet and unlock it the same way. There are several ways to secure your tablet to make it so you are the only one who can access your tablet. Open your app drawer by tapping the Apps icon in the top right of the screen. Locate your Settings and tap the app to open. From the Settings menu, locate the "Location & security" option. Scroll down on this page until you see settings for your lock screen. Right now, the option under "Lock screen" should say "Not secured," as shown in Figure 9–1. Tap

"Configure lock screen" to change this. Choose whichever option suits you best from among the following options:

- *Off*: This will remove the lock screen entirely, making it so the device is ready to be used as soon as you wake it by pressing your power button.

- *Not secured*: This is the current setting, which enables a basic lock screen that will allow you to move the lock bubble out of the ring to unlock the device.

- *Pattern*: This security measure allows you to protect your device by requiring a pattern that you have designed in order to unlock the device. If you tap Pattern, you will be walked through the process of setting up your pattern.

- *PIN*: Securing your tablet with a PIN will make it so you can access the tablet only by entering a PIN of your choosing. The PIN can be as many digits as you choose, but it must be at least four digits long.

- *Password*: Similar to how you would secure your computer, you have the option to unlock your device with a password of your choosing so that only someone with the password would be able to unlock the tablet.

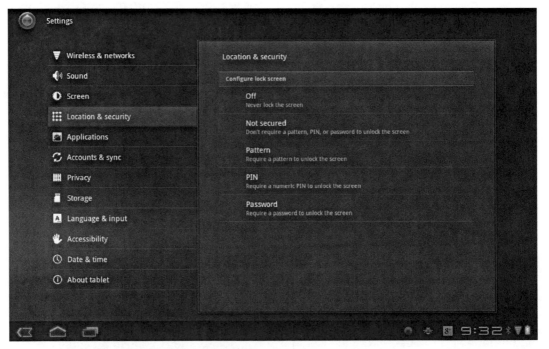

Figure 9–1. *Configuring the lock screen in Honeycomb*

Letting Others Know You're the Owner (and How to Contact You)

In addition to securing your tablet, you have the option to leave information for someone who may pick up your tablet in an attempt to use it. Right underneath the "Configure lock screen" function you will see the owner information. Tap "owner info" to reveal the ability to leave a message on your lock screen, as shown in Figure 9–2, for anybody who could stumble across it.

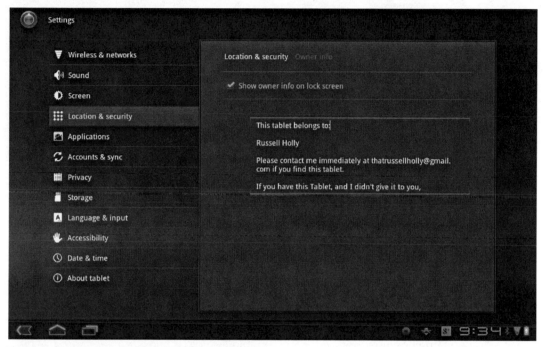

Figure 9–2. *Owner info screen in Honeycomb*

You have quite a bit of room here, at least eight lines of text if you are using a 10-inch tablet, so feel free to put whatever you would like here as a message. Once you have written anything in this field, the changes will be reflected immediately on your lock screen, as shown in Figure 9–3.

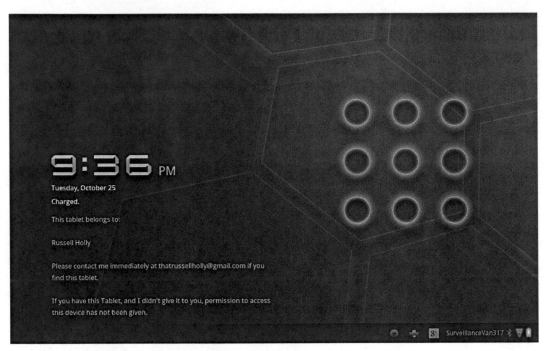

Figure 9–3. *Pattern lock screen with owner info in Honeycomb*

This is a pretty surefire way to keep most people out of your tablet, but just like with a computer, there are ways to bypass this. Your Android tablet can offer additional security when you are using a computer other than your own.

Securing Your Google Account

Another tool you can use to secure not only your tablet but also your Gmail account when you use Gmail on your computer is to enable Google's *two-step verification*. This utility will enable you to secure your account using your password as well as a code that is randomly generated every couple of seconds, making it very difficult to break into your account.

Start by logging into your Gmail account on your computer. In the top-right corner of the screen you will see an avatar to the left of the gear. Click this icon to open the Google Account menu, and select Account Settings. From Account Settings, select "Account overview," as shown in Figure 9–4. Select "Using 2-step verification" from the list that appears. You will be redirected to the setup page for two-step verification.

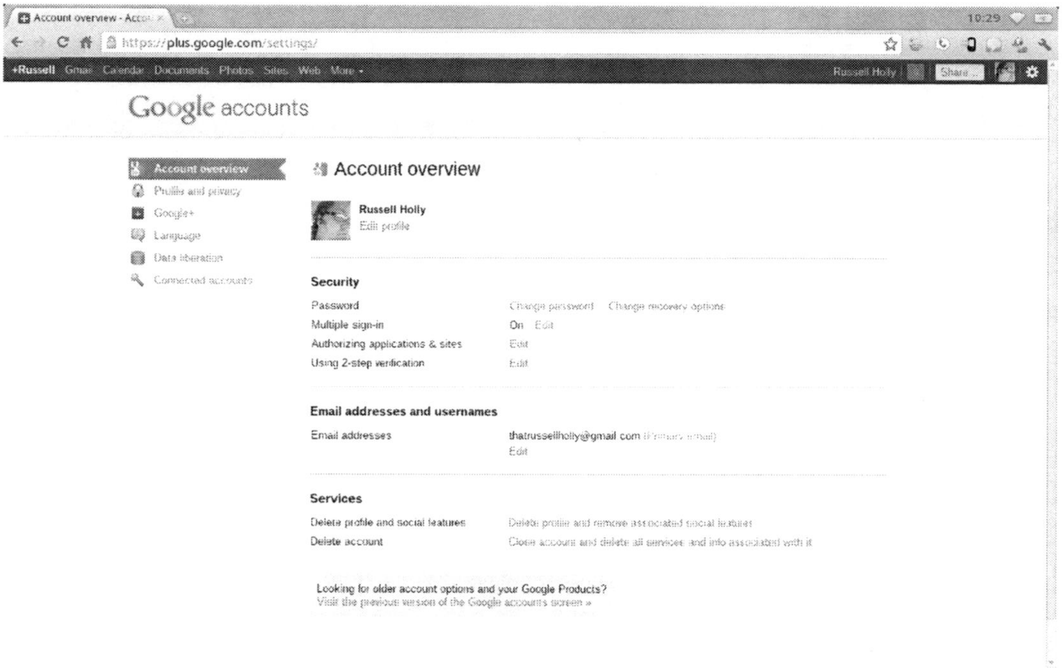

Figure 9–4. *Google account overview from the computer*

To enable two-step verification, you will need to give Google a phone number that it can either send a text message to or call and give you an authentication code. This step is to confirm that you are a human being and that you are aware this is happening to your account. Enter your preferred method of receiving the code and click "Send code," as shown in Figure 9–5. Within moments you will receive your code, which you now enter in step 2. When you have entered the code, click Verify, and Google will confirm you have completed this step. Once this step is finished, you will be able to activate two-step verification.

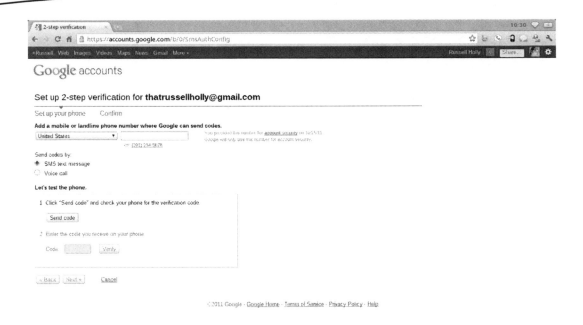

Figure 9–5. *Two-step verification setup from the computer*

Using your tablet, go to the Play Store and search for *Google Authenticator*. This is a free app from Google, so just tap Download and open the app when it finishes installing. The app will ask you to connect to your Google account using the code that was generated during the last step. Enter that code, and Google Authenticator will be ready to be used.

Now, any time you log in to your Gmail account from a new computer (and once every 30 days on your computer), you will be asked to log in using not only your password but also the randomly generated password from Google Authenticator, as shown in Figure 9–6.

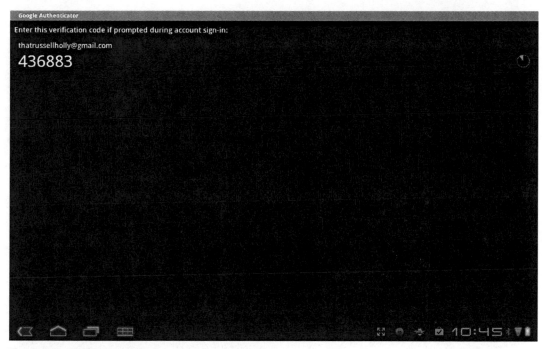

Figure 9–6. *Google Authenticator app in Honeycomb*

Encrypting Stored Information

There are a number of reasons a person would want to go the extra mile to secure their device. Maybe your company has sensitive or private information and will allow you to leave your office with that information only if it is secure. Maybe you've been a victim of identity theft and would like to be sure that your personal information is secure. Maybe you would like to avoid identity theft in the first place. Whatever your reason, if you would like to encrypt the information on your Android tablet, that option is available.

Locate your Settings app in the app drawer on the top left of your home screen. From the Settings menu, tap "Location & security." Scroll down until you see "Encrypt tablet" in the list and tap that option.

> **WARNING:** To move forward with encrypting your tablet, the device must be both fully charged and connected to a power source. If your device is currently running on battery power, you must connect the tablet to a power source and allow the device to fully charge . Additionally, you must have a lock-screen PIN or password set in order for the encryption to take place.

When you are ready to encrypt your device, select the Encrypt Tablet button shown in Figure 9–7. You will be asked to provide your security PIN or password to proceed. The tablet warns that this process can take an hour or more, and you cannot disturb the tablet while it reboots and continues the encryption process. When the operation is complete, you will be invited to enter your PIN or password every time the tablet boots.

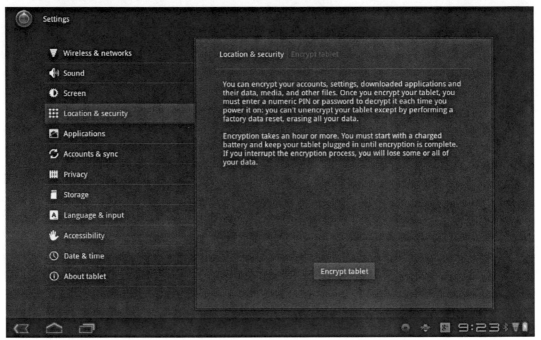

Figure 9–7. *Encrypt tablet view in Honeycomb*

Securing Your Proprietary Network Connections

Specific kinds of networks require a secured connection to access remotely. When trying to access those networks, it is often a requirement that the device you are using provides what is known as a *security credential* in order to access that network. This is common for offices that use virtual private networks (VPNs). If your office uses a VPN, you may be given a security certificate to install on your device in order to give your tablet access to the VPN. Android tablets offer a means of not only installing these certificates but also securing them on the device.

Installing a Security Certificate

If you need a security certificate, you first should acquire the certificate. Typically, whoever manages your VPN will be able to generate one. The certificate will need to be transferred to the tablet by either e-mail, MicroSD card, or USB. Once you have the certificate on your device, you are ready to install.

Locate your Settings app in the app drawer on the top left of your home screen. From the Settings menu, tap "Location & security." Scroll down until you see Credential Storage. Select Install from the list shown in Figure 9–8. If your tablet detects more than one certificate, you will be asked to choose which you would like to install. If you have only one certificate, the installation process will begin. This process should take only a moment if the certificate is accepted, greeting you with an "Installation Successful" pop-up. If the installation was unsuccessful, you will need to contact the author of your certificate for the correct certificate.

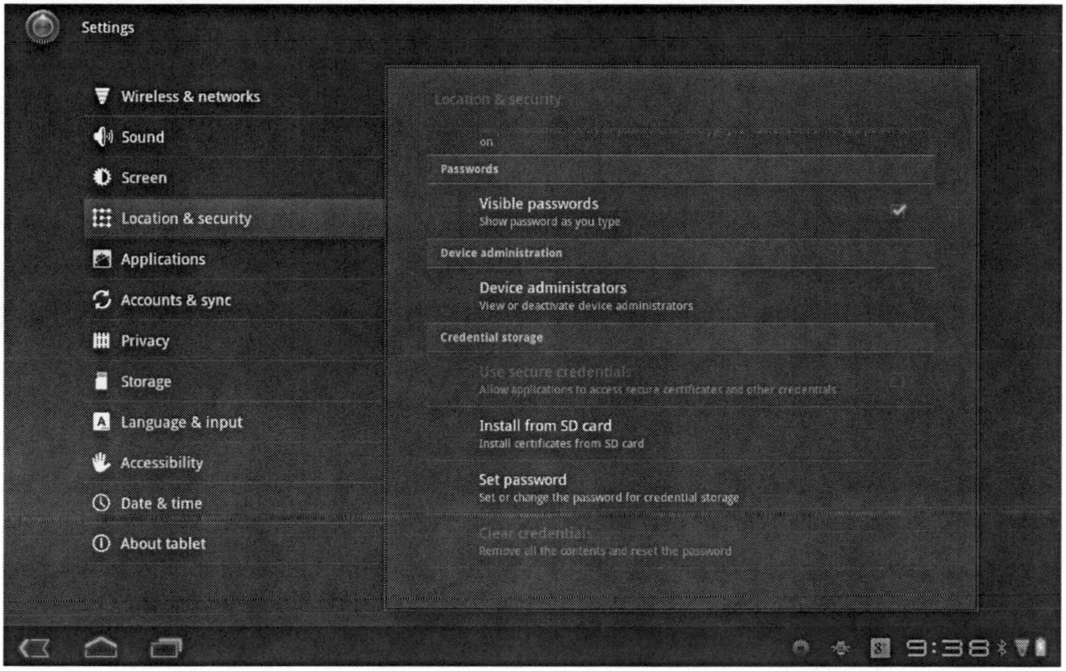

Figure 9–8. *Credential storage view in Honeycomb*

Above the Install option, the "Use secure credentials" option will no longer be gray, giving you the option to activate the secure credentials by tapping the check box. Once this box is lit, you will be able to use your secure connection. While this option is lit, there will be an icon in your notification tray. Tapping that icon will bring you back to this Settings menu to allow you to quickly disable the use of the certificate.

Protecting Your Certificate with a Password

As an added security measure, you are able to place a password on the folder that stores your security certificate in case your MicroSD card is liberated from your device or the folder is somehow extracted from your tablet.

Locate your Settings app in the app drawer on the top left of your home screen. From the Settings menu, tap "Location & security." Scroll down until you see Credential Storage, and select "Set password." A password box will appear, asking you to create an eight-character (or more) password for your secure credentials folder on your tablet. As shown in Figure 9–9, enter the password, and then confirm the password in the field beneath it. When you are finished, tap OK.

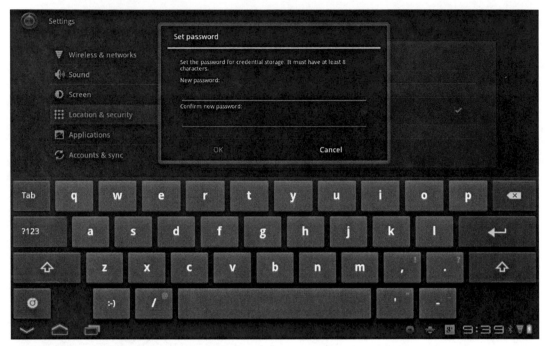

Figure 9–9. *Password-protect credentials in Honeycomb*

If you need security credentials for your work, your Android tablet is prepared to not only offer that feature but also keep it secure as your personal device. By being able to secure the device yourself, you can often avoid the need for your employer to administer the device directly.

Empowering Your System Administrator

If the primary purpose of your Android tablet is for work or if your Android tablet was issued to you as a work device, there is likely a need for remote device administration. Remote administration is a way for Android devices to receive additional security protocols from your administrator. Additionally, it grants the administrator the ability to remotely locate a device or wipe all the data off of the tablet in case of theft.

> **NOTE:** Device administration applies only to Google Apps account users. This is typically a tool used by companies that use Google for their e-mail or documents. If you are not a Google Apps user, this does not apply to you.

To enable this service, head to the Play Store either from the app or from the Play Store shortcut to the right of the app drawer. Tap the Search icon and search for *Google Apps Device Policy*. This is a free app from Google, so tap Install and open the app when it has finished installing.

When the app is installed, you will be prompted to activate the device administrator. A policy warning appears and informs you that this will enable the remote administrator to do the following:

- Erase all data without warning, via a factory reset

- Change the screen-unlock password

- Set specific rules for the passwords that users are allowed to generate

- Count the number of times a password is entered in incorrectly, allowing you to permanently lock the device if too many failed attempts occur

- Control how and when the screen locks

- Require that stored app data be encrypted

Administrators will access these features from within the control panel on their Google Apps account. These added measures will ensure your tablet is as secure as possible and help stop would-be intruders from accessing sensitive data.

Summary

Your Android tablet can be a powerful tool in the workplace, provided you have the security measures in place to keep your data intact and you know what to do in the event that anything happens to your tablet. These steps will keep your information safe from just about anything.

In the next chapter, you will learn about keeping your data stored using cloud computing and the storage utilities on your Android tablet.

Chapter 10

Harnessing "the Cloud" on Your Tablet

As capable as your Android tablet is, the device is limited when compared to a laptop or a desktop in many ways. For starters, there's not nearly as much storage or RAM in a tablet as you're likely to find in a traditional computer. Additionally, the processor for your traditional computer is going to be much faster. Many apps on your Android tablet have gotten around both limitations by sharing the work of specific tasks with remote computers over an Internet connection. This use of computers other than your tablet, and often located within immense "farms" of computers, is called *cloud computing*.

In this chapter, you will learn about some of the ways that cloud computing and cloud storage are used to increase the performance of your Android tablet.

Storing Your Data in the Cloud

In Chapter 8, we briefly covered a utility named Dropbox, which allowed the use of cloud storage to access files from your computer. This is an excellent utility if you do a lot of your work from your computer, but the software is limited when it comes to automatically sharing files from your tablet back to your Dropbox folder. In this section, you'll see some of the applications that make it easy to sync the data on your tablet with data stored in the cloud.

Storing Data with SugarSync

The ability to store files in the cloud is a valuable tool to have at your disposal, especially on a device with a limited amount of storage. (Even with expansion MicroSD cards or SD card adapters, the most storage you can hope for is 128GB, which is also very expensive.) Being able to detect when there is a new photo, document, and so on, and be able to automatically sync that file with your account is significant. That feature in particular is a strong suit of the SugarSync service.

The SugarSync app is free in the Play Store, and you can locate the app by searching for *SugarSync*. Tap the Download button to install, and tap Open when the installation is finished. Since SugarSync is an online service where your information will be kept, it is necessary for you to create an account with SugarSync. When you open the application, the first thing you will be prompted to do is create an account. Follow the instructions here to create your SugarSync account.

Once you have successfully logged into SugarSync, you will be asked if you would like to sync your files, as shown in Figure 10–1, with a note that any additional photos you take will be uploaded to the SugarSync service in the background, meaning it will do so without telling you. You can choose to begin this process now, activate the feature now, or choose not to use it at all. If you choose to begin the process now, you will be asked if you want SugarSync to also perform background updates while on a mobile network. This applies to you only if you pay for a monthly mobile data plan.

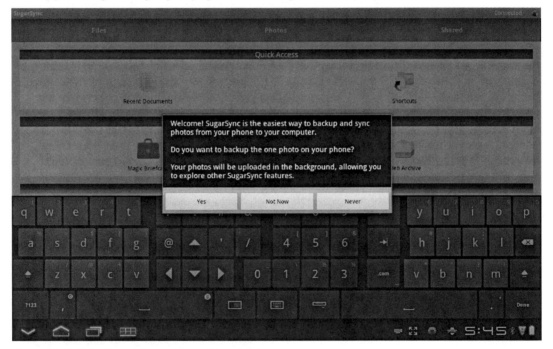

Figure 10–1. *SugarSync setup screen on Honeycomb*

Once you have decided how you want SugarSync to work, the main menu for the service appears. From this page, as shown in Figure 10–2, you can view and download files from any other device you have attached to your account or choose additional files or folders to upload to the service. To do this, locate the device you are currently on in the My Devices section. From here you will be given a basic file manager, shown in Figure 10–3, that you can navigate by scrolling and tapping. If you choose, you can press and hold on a single file or folder, which will cause a menu to pop up and ask you if you would like to sync this file or folder to your account. Once you have chosen to sync a folder, SugarSync will ask you if the app should consistently scan that folder and upload new items that appear in the folder.

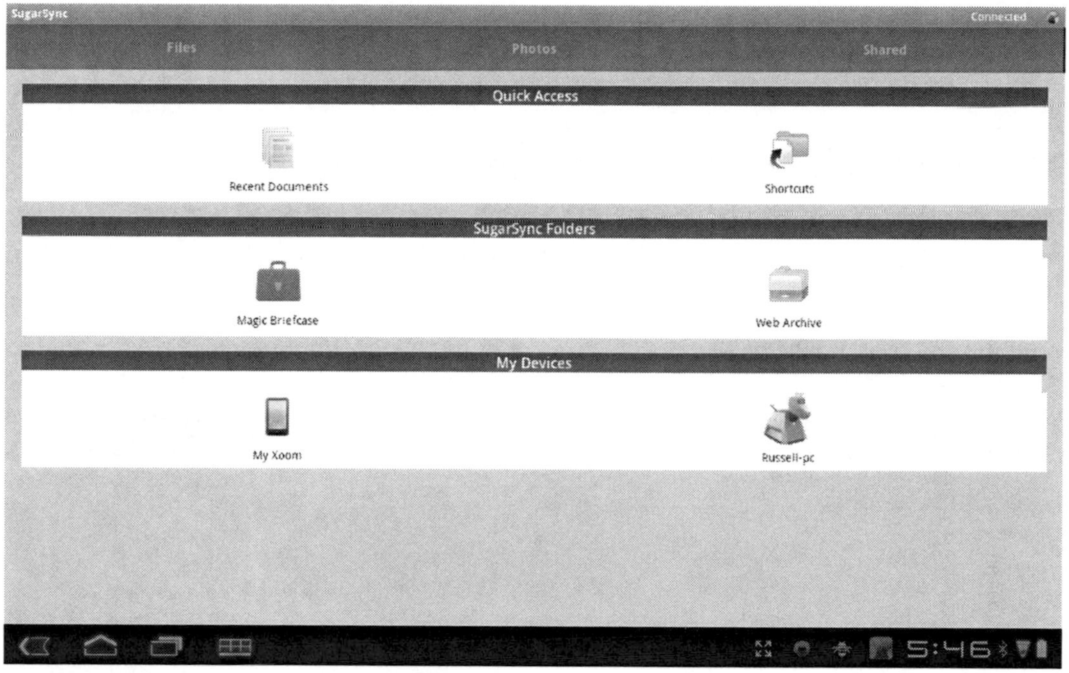

Figure 10–2. *SugarSync main menu on Honeycomb*

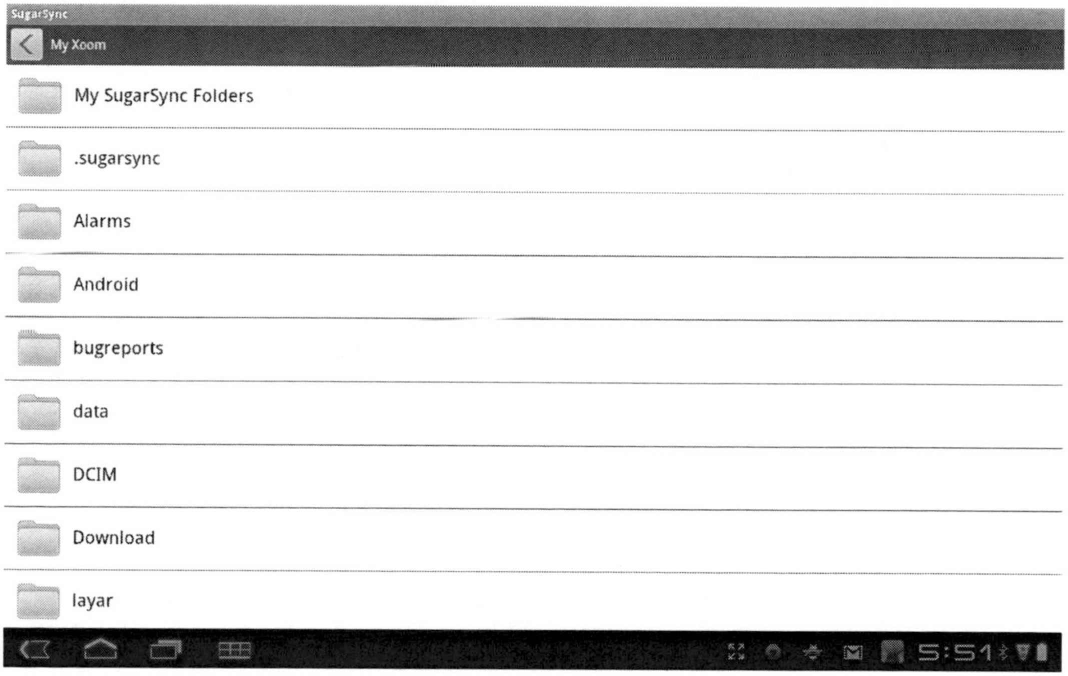

Figure 10–3. *SugarSync file manager on Honeycomb*

SugarSync takes the process of remembering to upload every new file you have out of the equation if you choose to let it. This service can do much of the heavy lifting for you when it comes to preserving your pictures and files, and it can do all of it automatically.

Managing Word Documents with Google Docs

While we already discussed how to use Google Docs in Chapter 3, it is worth mentioning again that this is a perfect example of utilizing the cloud for your personal use. Google Docs is, first and foremost, an online service. Google Docs is a word processor built for use in a web browser. The app for Android, shown in Figure 10–4, enables you to not only access but also edit and create new documents and save them to the cloud from the moment you start working in them.

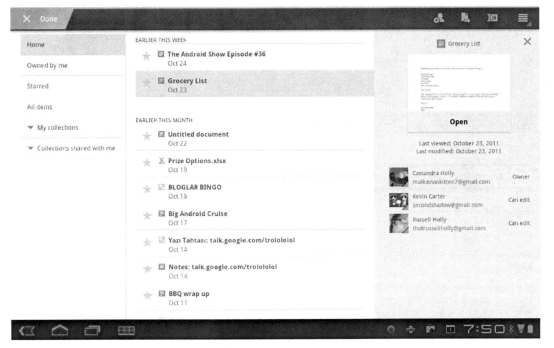

Figure 10–4. *Google Docs home screen on Honeycomb*

Computing with Cloud-Provided Services

The term *cloud computing* is most commonly used to describe services that exist entirely online. A perfect example of this concept is Google Music. No matter where you are, you can access the same service with the same music. When it comes to your tablet, however, cloud computing can be used to assist in operations that require more power than your tablet has to offer.

Searching for Images with Google Goggles

When you search for something, you enter the most accurate description of something, click Search, and browse the results in hopes that your description was good enough to get the result you wanted. This is really easy to do as long as you are searching for something easy to describe, but it's not always so easy. Google suggests it might be easier to find more accurate information about something if you could just take a picture of it. Google Goggles allows you to take a picture of anything and search using that picture instead of words.

The Google Goggles app is free in the Android Market; just search *Goggles* in the Market. Tap Download to install the app and tap Open when the app has finished installing. When you open the app, you will be given a basic tutorial on the things you are able to do with Google Goggles. Searching by picture isn't its only trick; it can also do the following:

- *Translate text*: Take a photo of the text in another language and Goggles will translate it.

- *Solve sudoku puzzles*: Take a photo of a Sudoku puzzle, and Goggles will return with the solution to the puzzle.

- *Save business cards*: Take a photo of a business card with Goggles, and you will be able to store that information as a new Gmail contact.

- *Scan bar codes*: Snap a photo of a normal bar code or a QRCode, and Goggles will search the Internet for the result. In the case of QRCodes, Goggles will take you to the web site or file that QRCode is pointing to.

When you are ready to take a photo, you will be given a screen similar to your Camera app. If you are scanning a bar code, like the one in Figure 10–5, the app will detect the bar code and search automatically; there's no need to take a picture. For everything else, hold the tablet steady and take your picture when ready. As soon as this happens, you will see a light pass over the image back and forth, as shown in Figure 10–6, as Google scans the information in the picture. When the results are ready, the app will take you to a Google search results page or to complete one of the previously mentioned tasks depending on the image.

Figure 10–5. *QRCode scanning Google Goggles for Honeycomb*

Figure 10–6. *Google Goggles image scan in Honeycomb*

Goggles makes several kinds of jobs easier by sending the hard work to the Internet to find the right answer.

Accessing Your Home Data Storage with Wyse PocketCloud

Syncing your files back and forth between your home computer and your tablet can be easy enough, but many people still use their home computers to store massive amounts of information. Many of these services give you only 2GB of storage for free, and while that is a great convenience to have, it may seem unnecessary to some to pay for storage online when their computer at home already has hundreds of gigabytes of storage. Additionally, if you are working with large files of any kind, it is not a fast process to move those files from your computer to your tablet, especially if you are using a mobile network where you are limited on how much bandwidth you can use. The team at Wyse created PocketCloud to solve this problem. PocketCloud allows you to use your tablet to not only see but completely control your computer remotely.

PocketCloud is offered in both a paid version and a free version. The free version will allow you to access your computer using Wyse's remote connection services, while the paid version offers significant performance increases and additional features by using Wyse's cloud computing system to enhance the experience. Additionally, the paid version will allow you to transfer files directly to the tablet, as well as play a video or audio file from the tablet over the Internet. If you choose to install the free version, it is very easy to upgrade to the paid version if you feel like you will use the service frequently.

The first time you open the PocketCloud app, you are invited to a guided tour of setting up PocketCloud, as shown in Figure 10–7. It will be important for you to be at your computer for the setup, because it involves installing software on your computer. Once the setup process is complete, you will be prompted to sign in to the app using your Google account. This will scan the PocketCloud network for any computers that are also connected to the service with your Google account and pair the connections automatically.

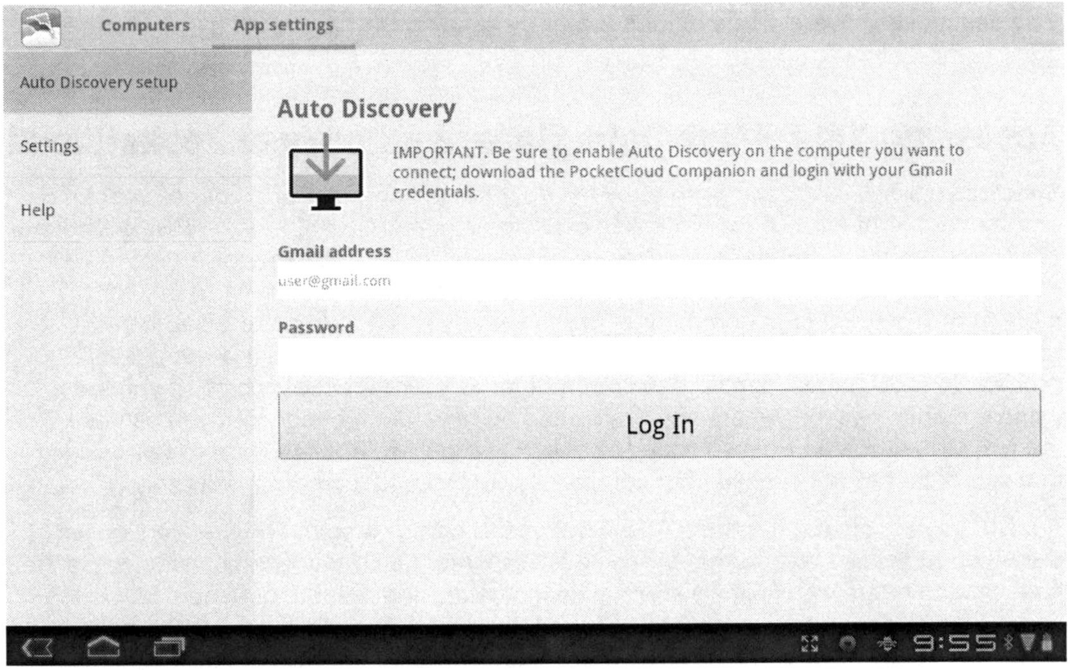

Figure 10–7. *Wyse PocketCloud autodiscovery screen in Honeycomb*

Once you select Connect, the screen will immediately begin to show you what you have on your desktop, as shown in Figure 10–8. From this point, you will be able to access your desktop from anywhere with an Internet connection. The slower the internet connection, however, the slower the computer at home will respond. In the paid version of this app, the PocketCloud servers store a virtual copy of your desktop in the cloud to make this experience much faster.

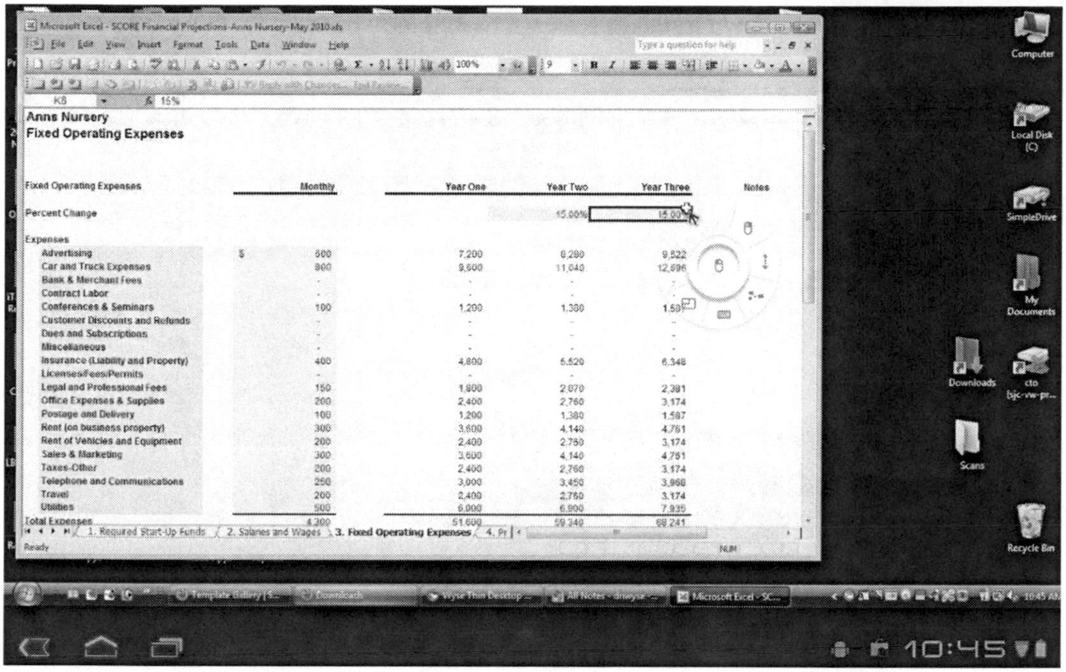

Figure 10–8. *Wyse PocketCloud desktop view in Honeycomb*

Speeding Up Internet Browsing with Opera Mini Browser

When browsing the Internet on a mobile device like a tablet, large web sites or web sites with a lot of interactive content can often slow down the browsing experience. The processor and the browser on your tablet can't handle the volume of the information it is receiving, or sometimes the information is not presented in a format the tablet browser can deal with. In these cases, it would be beneficial if the browser was able to somehow give the job of processing that content to the cloud, so the information could be presented in a format that is easier for the tablet to handle. This is exactly what the Opera Mini Browser does for you.

The Opera Mini browser is a free app found in the Play Store. Search for *Opera Mini* in the Play Store, and tap Download. When the app has finished installing, tap Open. Opera will ask that you agree to its terms of service before you start using the browser. If you agree to the terms presented, tap Accept in the bottom-left corner of the app.

If you are used to the Android browser, you will notice some significant differences in the way Opera works. For starters, the start page shown in Figure 10–9 offers a grid of web sites that you have been to before to make it easy to return to those web sites. Just tap one of the squares inside the grid, and the page will begin to load. Opera Mini observes all of your web traffic through its app and will automatically compress images and adjust the font size of incoming web sites, which will give the tablet far less work to do in trying to present the web page to you. Opera Mini does not currently support the ability to deliver content that was created using Flash, a technology commonly used in heavily interactive web sites.

Figure 10–9. *Opera Mini Browser start screen in Honeycomb*

Opera Mini is perfect for when you are on the go or are using mobile broadband to surf the Web; even on a slower Internet connection Opera Mini will load many pages faster than the Android browser, because of its ability to compress images before they get to you.

Summary

The term *cloud computing* refers to an incredibly wide variety of technologies, but you can use those technologies to get much more out of your Android tablet. Not only are many of Google's services almost entirely cloud based, but more and more companies are following Google's lead every day. In the next chapter, you will learn about the risks and benefits behind gaining access to a deeper level of control of your Android tablet, via a process called *rooting*.

Chapter 11

Customizing Your Android Tablet

If you're like most tablet owners, it's important to you that the device feels like it's yours. Right now, you have the same background wallpaper, same virtual keyboard, and same everything as anybody else. But there are tools at your disposal that can separate you from the crowd, as well as provide a better way to accomplish basic tasks on your tablet.

In this chapter, we'll look at two ways to customize your computer. First we'll look ways to modify the virtual keyboard that ships with your tablet, and then we'll see how to modify its home screen.

Customizing the Keyboard

Likely the most important part of your experience on any Android tablet is the virtual keyboard. If you do not like the keyboard on your tablet, you are not likely to use it very often. You need a keyboard that suits you in order to enjoy the tablet experience. For some, the stock keyboard on their tablet might not be a great experience. Fortunately, this is something Android makes really easy to replace. All you need to do is search the Play Store and choose a keyboard that suits you better. Two of the most popular choices are Thumb Keyboard and Flex T9.

Putting the Keyboard Within Reach of Your Thumbs

If you have a 10-inch tablet, it's not easy to use your thumbs while you're holding the device in landscape mode. The virtual keyboard stretches across the entire width of the tablet, making it difficult to reach its middle characters. You could type with one hand and hold the tablet with the other, but that would be much slower. Thumb Keyboard separates the keyboard right down the middle and shoves its left and right halves toward the edges of the tablet, bringing them within reach of your thumbs.

Thumb Keyboard is not a free application. Purchase the app in the Play Store if you think this is the kind of keyboard you want to use. Tap Purchase and complete the instructions given; then exit the Play Store when the app has finished installing. Unlike most apps, you won't open Thumb Keyboard once it's installed, because it is a component of the Android operating system.

From the home screen, tap the Apps icon on the top right of the screen and search for your Settings app. In your Settings menu, locate "Language & input" toward the middle of the screen and tap. Swipe to the bottom of the menu that opens, and there you will find Keyboard Settings, as shown in Figure 11–1. To activate Thumb Keyboard, you will need to tap "Configure input methods" and allow Thumb Keyboard to act as a replacement for your keyboard.

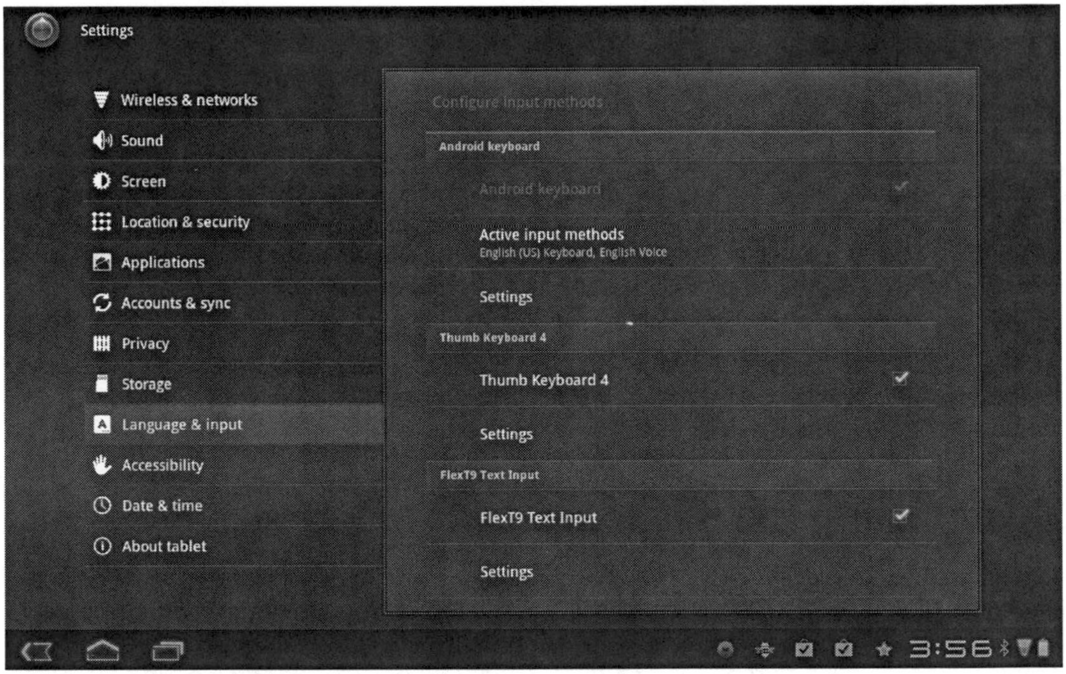

Figure 11–1. *Keyboard settings in Honeycomb*

All installed keyboards will appear in the "Select input method" list; simply tap the check box next to Thumb Keyboard, as shown in Figure 11–2. When the green dot appears, you will be able to use Thumb Keyboard. Additionally, if you would like to adjust any of the settings for Thumb Keyboard, you would do so here under Settings in the Thumb Keyboard menu. Tab the back arrow to be taken to the previous menu.

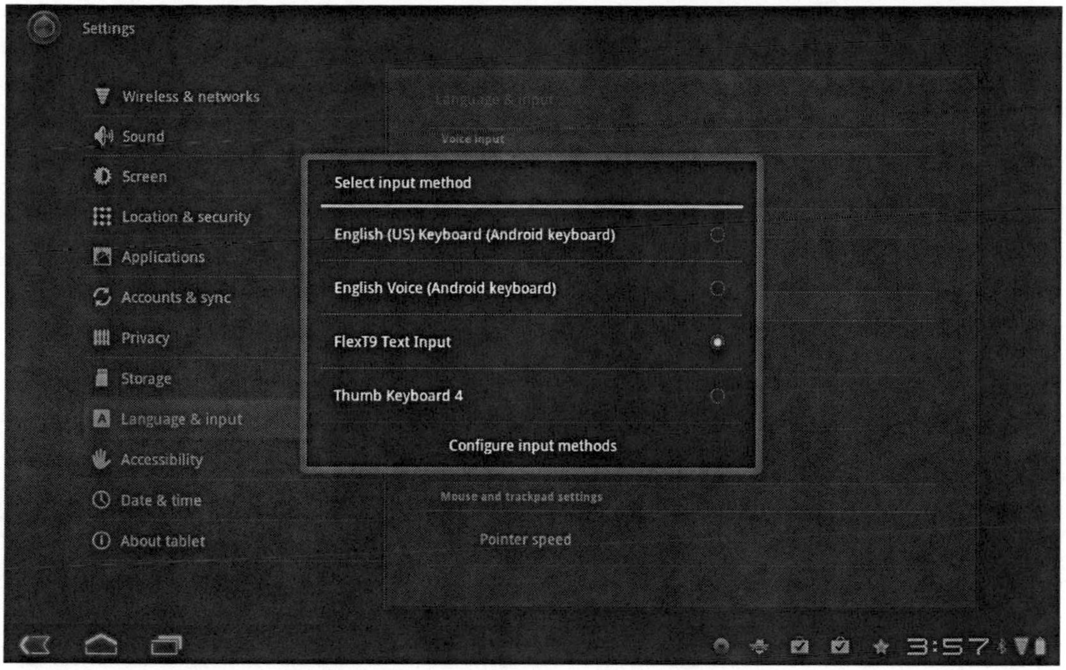

Figure 11–2. *Input select screen with multiple keyboards*

Just above the previous selection, we now need to tap "Current input method." A menu will pop up asking you to choose which keyboard you would like to use. Select Thumb Keyboard, and then tap the home button. From this point on, any time you need a keyboard, Thumb Keyboard will be what appears, as shown in Figure 11–3.

Figure 11–3. *Thumb Keyboard for tablets*

Accepting Handwritten and Voice Input

As long as we have been entering information on computers, there have been companies that have tried to improve the method in which we input that information. When digital pocket devices became popular, there was even a push to use your handwriting to input information. Later, there was eventually a voice translator that allowed you to simply speak and the words would appear on the screen. It is the gift of variety that is offered with the Flex T9 keyboard. You can choose to use voice to text, use handwriting, or simply type on the keyboard in order to put words on the screen.

Flex T9, as shown in Figure 11–4, is not a free app, but you can find it in the Android Market. Follow the instructions for activating Flex T9 on your tablet. From the home screen, tap the Apps icon on the top right of the screen and search for your Settings app. Inside your Settings menu, locate "Language & input" toward the middle of the screen and tap. Toward the bottom of the menu that opens, you will find Keyboard Settings. To activate Flex T9, you will need to tap "Configure input method" and allow Flex T9 to act as a replacement for your keyboard.

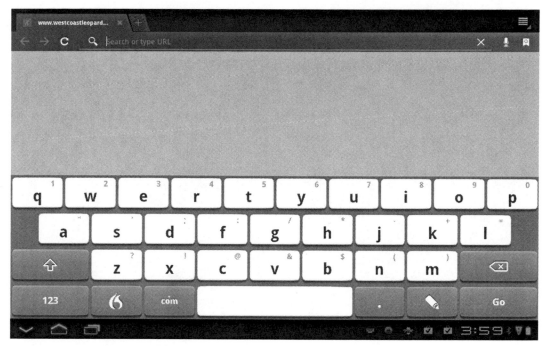

Figure 11–4. *Flex T9 keyboard for tablets*

All installed keyboards will appear on this list; simply tap the check box next to Flex T9. When the check mark appears, you will be able to use Flex T9. Additionally, if you would like to adjust any of the settings for Flex T9, you would do so here under Settings in the Flex T9 menu. Tab the back arrow to be taken to the previous menu.

Just above the previous selection, we now need to tap "Current Input method." A menu will pop up asking you to choose which keyboard you would like to choose. Select Flex T9, and then tap the home button. From this point on, any time you need a keyboard, Flex T9 will be what appears.

Using Flex T9 as your keyboard of choice is easy, but you can also use it to talk directly to the tablet and have the words be translated into text. Tap the flame on the keyboard, and a vocalize option will appear on the screen, as shown in Figure 11–5. When you have finished talking the sentence you wanted to say, tap the vocalizer, and the translation will appear on the screen. Additionally, if you tap the pencil instead, you will be able to draw the letters individually on the screen, and they will appear as though you had typed them.

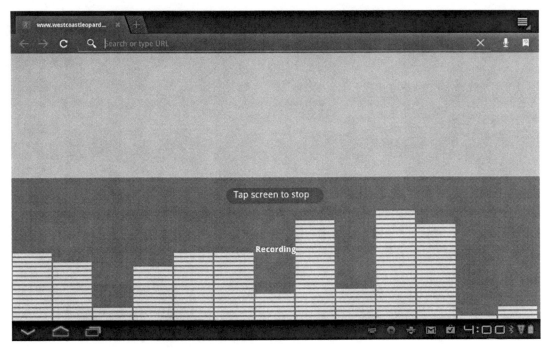

Figure 11–5. *Voice translation on Flex T9 for tablets*

Customizing Your Home Screen

You are able to customize just about anything in Android to suit you. The home screen was made for you to place whatever apps or widgets you want on the screen and be able to enjoy the experience as your own. However, there are a couple of things you are able to customize that require the help of other apps. This is where projects like ADW Launcher come in. Instead of allowing you to customize a single element, ADW Launcher allows you to replace the entire home screen with a new experience altogether.

Go to the Android Market and search for *ADW Launcher*. ADW Launcher is a free app in the Market but offers an update with additional features called ADW EX. Pick whichever one you like and install it. When you are finished, tap the home button. You will be prompted to choose between ADW Launcher and the Launcher that comes with Android. Tap ADW Launcher. This pop-up message asking you which Launcher app you would prefer to use will now appear every time you tap the home key, as shown in Figure 11–6. If you decide you would like to stick with ADW, you can check the box that says "Use by default for this action," and the message will not pop up anymore.

Figure 11–6. *Launcher selection screen in Honeycomb*

ADW Launcher looks and feels pretty different from the Launcher you have been using so far. For starters, your Apps button is on the top left, not the top right. The top right now has some small quick-access buttons for you. You can quickly add to the home screen with the plus button, change your wallpaper with the wallpaper button, search the tablet, change the number of home screen windows you have, and quickly access your settings.

The next thing you will notice is the bar, shown in Figure 11–7, going across the bottom of your home screen. This is a dock, similar to one you would see in Windows 7 or Apple's OS X. You can take apps and place them in the dock by dragging their icons down to the dock and dropping them. The dock stays with you, no matter what home screen window you are on. This way, if you have apps that you commonly use, you don't have to go looking for them.

Figure 11–7. *ADW Launcher EX on Honeycomb*

ADW Launcher has its own collection of settings. If you tap the Settings icon at the top right of your screen, you will see ADW Settings, as shown in Figure 11–8. Tapping this menu item will show you all of the features you can customize with ADW Launcher. You can adjust how apps look inside the app drawer or how large the icons in the dock bar are. You can even change how many columns and rows there are on your home screen, allowing you to fit as few or as many apps and widgets there as you like. As impressive as the ability to change features is, the real ability to customize ADW Launcher comes from the ability to theme your ADW experience with ADW themes.

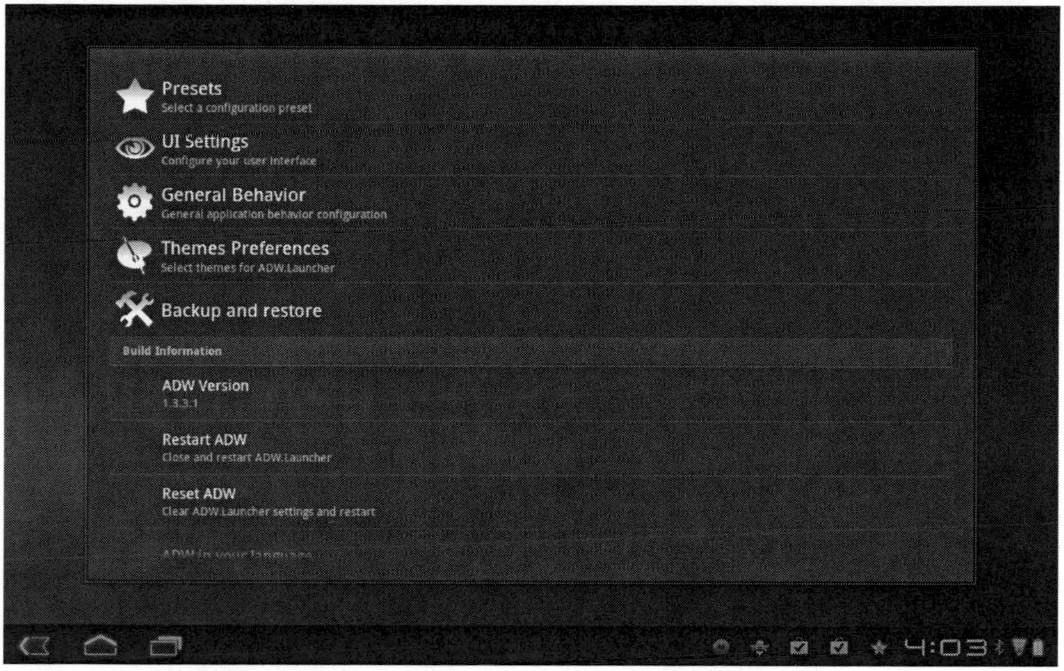

Figure 11–8. *ADW Launcher EX Settings menu*

Tap the Themes and Preferences option in the ADW Settings menu, and you will be asked to either install an existing theme or get a new one. Tap Get Themes! and you will be taken to the Android Market to see the collection. Hundreds of developers have collaborated to create different themes for your tablet with ADW Launcher. Pick any of the ADW themes and install them just as you would an app, as shown in Figure 11–9. When the theme has finished installing, press the back key to return to the ADW Launcher Settings menu.

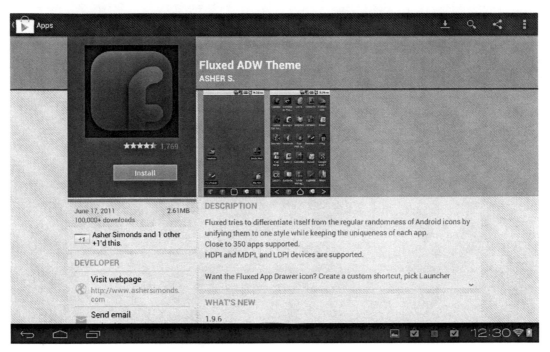

Figure 11-9. *ADW theme Fluxed in the Play Store*

You will now see the theme you installed with the stock ADW theme. Tap the theme you would like to activate and tap Install Theme. ADW Launcher will respond by asking you whether you would like to change the wallpaper to the one suggested by the theme. This is not a requirement; if you tap the Home button, you will see that your theme has been installed.

If you would ever like to go back to the home screen that your tablet came with, you can either uninstall ADW Launcher or head to the Settings menu. From the Settings menu, tap the Applications menu and tap "Manage applications." Find ADW Launcher in the list and tap to reveal the management options for this app. Scroll until you see "Launch by default." Here you will see an option labeled "Clear defaults." Tap it, as shown in Figure 11-10, and press the home button, where you will once again be prompted to choose which launcher you would like to use.

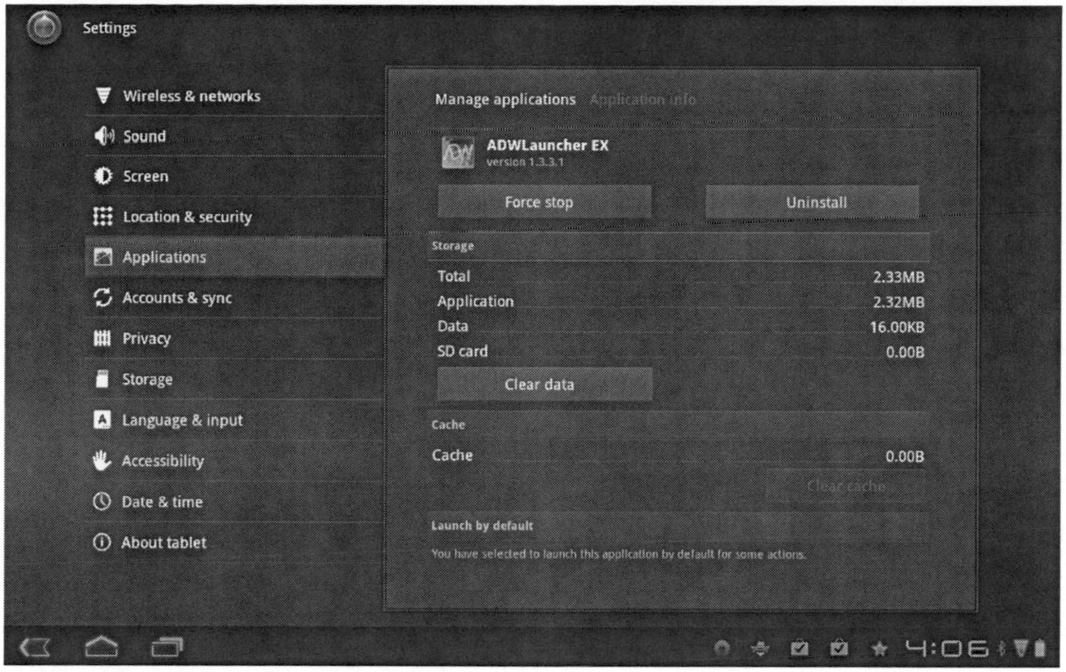

Figure 11–10. *Resetting Launcher defaults in Honeycomb*

Summary

Customization is an important part of using any device. So many people buy personalized accessories for a lot of things. Cases for phones, steering wheel covers, decorations in our homes...they all become a personalized extension of our ownership. It only makes sense that the same level of personalization would be available on a device you plan to use every day.

In the next chapter, you will learn how to take that customization much further by rooting your tablet and gaining access to the more technical parts of Android.

Chapter 12

Rooting Your Tablet

You've gotten the hang of the basic concepts of using an Android tablet by now. You can enjoy all the music, movies, and games you could possibly want to enjoy. You can run your digital world from your tablet, everything from e-mail and instant messaging to Facebook and Twitter. There are those of you reading, however, who are no doubt looking for how you can push your Android tablet even further. These are the kinds of things that your Android tablet might not have been specifically designed for, but developers figured it out and have shared the ability to do these things with you. There's just one small thing you have to do first, and that is to *root* your tablet.

Android is built on an operating system called Linux. Like most forms of Linux, you can gain complete control of your operating system by changing the type of user you are from a normal user to a superuser. When you have granted yourself superuser access on an Android tablet, you are able to control every aspect of your tablet and run apps that are able to push the limits of your tablet. This is not a process that is accomplished by flipping a switch but rather one that involves altering critical components of your tablet. Once you have finished making those adjustments, a superuser app similar to any other app on your tablet will be called on to grant access to anything that requests the superuser function.

We'll begin this chapter with a look at how you can gain superuser status to the Android OS, after which we'll explore some of the cool things you can accomplish once you have it.

Getting Permission to Root

Not all Android tablets are created equal. It might be easy to achieve superuser access on your tablet, or it might not be something that has been figured out on your tablet yet. This process is entirely based on hackers who have the time and resources to figure it out and then publish how they accomplish this task online so you can re-create their accomplishment. Typically, you can easily find out whether your tablet has been rooted if you just Google *<Name of Tablet> rooted*. Once you know that you can root your tablet, you are ready to move forward.

CHECK YOUR WARRANTY

You need to check the warranty for your device to make sure rooting your device does not void it. For most devices, there is no issue; however, it is important that you know for sure before you attempt to root your tablet. Rooting your tablet is in no way illegal, but it is often frowned upon if you pay for a monthly mobile data plan, since in some cases it is possible to use superuser status to share your Internet connection with other devices without paying for it.

There are forums all over the Internet filled with users who figured out how to root a tablet and are also willing to offer suggestions to help you along. In no way are these groups licensed or have permission to support your tablet, but these are nonetheless groups of highly skilled individuals who are willing to help if you ask. The following are two of them that I recommend if you're looking for guidance on how to proceed.

XDA-Developers

The hackers, modders, themers, and developers who make up the XDA-Developers forums are some of the most active on the Internet. These forums are filled with users who are very familiar with the practice of rooting a tablet and usually have easy-to-follow step-by-step instructions on how to root your tablet. Head to XDA-Developers.com to see whether your tablet is on their list.

RootzWiki.com

More than just a traditional forum, RootzWiki has a list of best practices for rooting most of the tablets out there. This site also offers a traditional forum where you can ask questions and get help from experienced users, but the organization of the wiki makes it much easier to locate the best way to root your tablet.

Follow the instructions for your device explicitly, and you will come back with superuser access on your tablet. Congratulations! Now, what do you do with it?

Getting the Most from a Rooted Tablet

Once you have superuser access to your tablet, most notably accomplished by having the superuser app functional on your tablet, you can now start exploring the deeper parts of your tablet. First you will need a couple of apps to help you along the way.

Exploring the Files on Your Android with Terminal

Anyone familiar with one of the many flavors of the Linux operating system (on which Android is based) will appreciate the ability to have the terminal experience on a tablet. Terminal allows you to explore the complete file system for your tablet and all of the information that is kept within. For users who want to modify their existing tablet experience without a premade app of some kind, the terminal is your best way to explore from the tablet.

From the Terminal, you can access the superuser account the same way you would in a Linux terminal. When you start, you will be presented with $ at your command prompt. From here, type **su**, as shown in Figure 12–1, and press the Enter key. If you have superuser access, the & will turn into a #, and you will be able to navigate to folders that would be locked to normal users.

Figure 12–1. *Terminal app on Honeycomb*

Plenty of people have never used a Linux-style terminal before but would still like to explore the root file system and make changes. For that user, the Root File Explorer app in the Play Store will offer you the tools you are looking for.

Root File Explorer breaks the file system down in the familiar folder-style visual experience. Tap a folder to view its contents, and use the back key to return to the previous folder. Figure 12–2 shows a typical display.

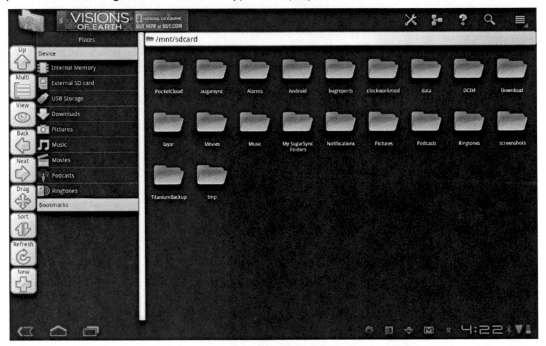

Figure 12–2. *Navigating through secured folders with the Root File Explorer*

Backing Up Your Device or Apps

You are going to be having some fun playing with the internals of your tablet, but all of the fun can come screeching to a halt if you break something and do not know how to fix it. There is an extremely easy solution once you have root access on your tablet. While Google provides you the ability to back up and sync your data from their apps (Gmail, Google Docs, Google Play Music), the same does not apply to any other apps on your tablet. So, you need something that can back up your data but also back up your entire tablet in case something goes wrong.

Perform a Backup and Restore with Rom Manager

It would provide significant peace of mind if you were able to just grab a *snapshot* (which is a backup) of your tablet as it is right now and save it in case you needed it. That way, if something breaks, you can just restore the backup and be good as new. The best way to do this on your Android tablet is with Rom Manager.

Install Rom Manager from the Android Market and open the app. The first thing you will be prompted to do is to set up your recovery to accept commands from Rom Manager. You will need to agree to this change in order to move forward. Rom Manager will replace the existing recovery system with one that was created by the team that made this app. Once this process is complete, you will have access to the app shown in Figure 12–3.

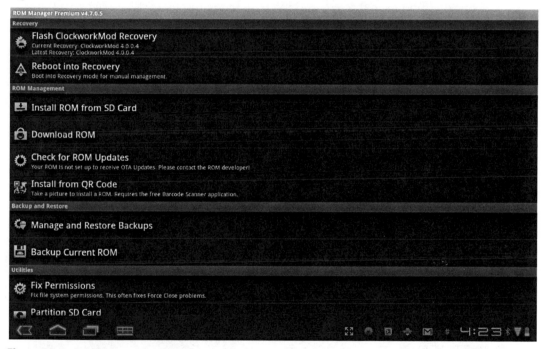

Figure 12–3. *Rom Manager for Android*

Scroll down until you find the Backup and Restore section of the app. From here, you can select Backup Current Rom. You will be prompted to name the backup. After you have named the backup, the tablet will reboot. For a full backup to happen, the tablet needs to be in the beginning part of the boot sequence. You will see the backup process begin, and a small bar on the bottom will fill as the backup takes place. When the backup is complete, the tablet will restart. Your backup has been saved to the storage on your tablet. For additional protection, copy the backup to your home or office computer so the backup is saved somewhere else.

Do Selective Backups with Titanium Backup

Backing up the entirety of your tablet is a great way to make sure your tablet experience is secured; you may not want to change your recovery because it may affect your warranty. So, you can back up all of your apps and your data using a less invasive kind of backup, called Titanium Backup. This app lets you pick and choose which apps and which data to back up.

Install Titanium Backup free from the Play Store. When the app opens, you will see three tabs across the top; tap the middle Backup/Restore tab. Here, you will see a list of the apps that are installed on your tablet, shown in Figure 12–4, and a comment on whether there is a backup of any of the apps in the list. Tap the app you want to back up, and a pop-up like the one in Figure 12–5 will appear asking you what you would like to do next. Tap backup, and save the app and the data to your backup. You will see a brief progress bar, followed by a completion notification.

Figure 12–4. *Titanium Backup selective backup*

Figure 12–5. *Titanium Backup individual app restore*

When you are finished backing up the apps you want archived, transfer this to your computer for safe keeping by connecting your tablet to the computer and transferring the files. When you need the files, move them back to the tablet. When you want to restore an app or data from an app, tap the app in the list and select Restore.

Taking a Screenshot

There's so much you can do with your Android tablet, but unless you are sitting next to someone else who cares, you are only able to enjoy the tablet by yourself for the most part. With a rooted Android tablet, you can take a screenshot of whatever you are doing on your tablet at the time and share it with the world just like you would any other picture.

Screenshot is available for free in the Play Store. After you have installed the app, you can open it to access some settings, shown in Figure 12–6. You can choose to set the quality of the picture and how the screenshot is taken. I have set it to take a picture after a five-second delay and to give me a button on the notification tray so I can quickly take a screenshot whenever I want.

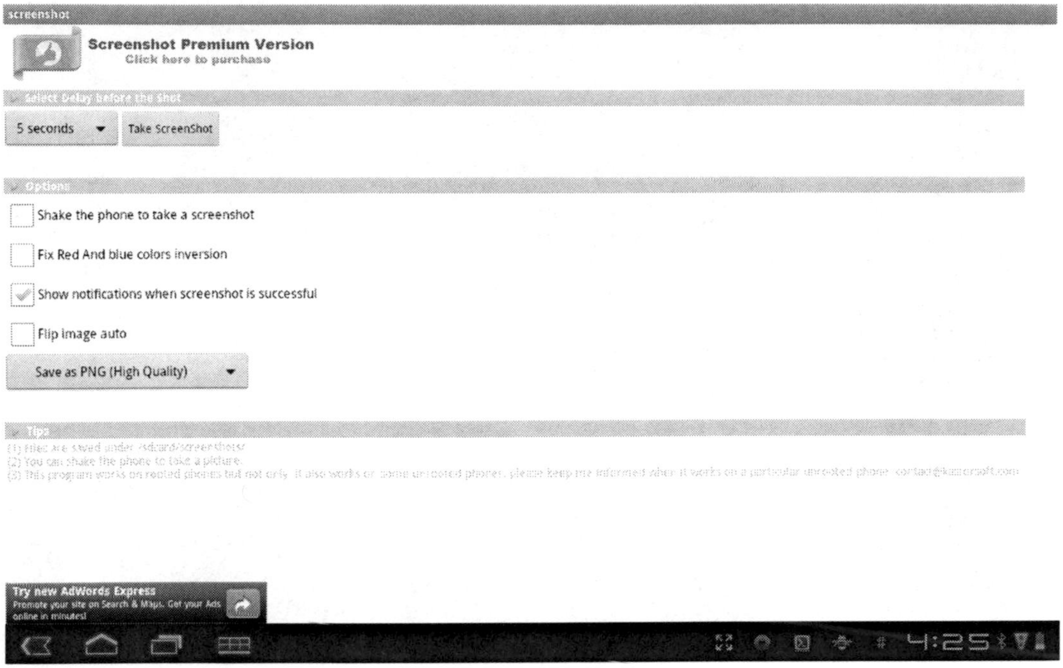

Figure 12–6. *Screenshot app for Honeycomb tablets*

When you do take a screenshot, you will be presented with a screen asking you how you want to save it, shown in Figure 12–7, and if you are ready to share it with the world or not.

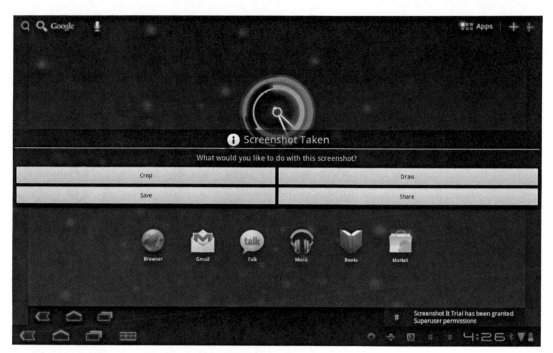

Figure 12–7. *Screenshot saves menu in Honeycomb Screenshot app*

Summary

Rooting a tablet is not for everyone. If it were, Google would release Android to us with root access included. By granting that power to ourselves, we take responsibility for our device in a whole new way. There are many who view this level of control over their device as the only way you truly "own" it.

Chapter 13

Using Amazon Apps

Because more people than ever on using the Internet for shopping, Amazon.com has become a household name. The assortment of items that can be found on Amazon is unparalleled, and its frequent buyer program, Amazon Prime, encourages more shopping there every day. Users who are comfortable shopping online are also becoming comfortable buying movies, books, and video games from a digital retailer. Amazon applied the iTunes music store concept to its own business model and started moving its massive book library to the digital/e-book space. Shortly afterward, Amazon announced the Kindle, a black-and-white e-book reader with great battery life that could carry hundreds of thousands of books and was connected right to Amazon.com for purchasing books.

The success of the Kindle led Amazon to expand its business to include digital stores for music, movies, and eventually apps for smartphones. The Kindle app and Amazon App Store are now available for every Android device on the market. These services can be installed separately, and they give any Android device access to the massive library of content Amazon has collected across these services. With a new arsenal of digital products, Amazon released the color Kindle Fire to support all of its existing services, plus a few new ones.

The Kindle Fire is a tablet running the Android operating system but has been heavily modified by Amazon to replace as many of Google's products and services with apps made and controlled by Amazon. Because of this, the Kindle Fire does not run any of the Google apps that were demonstrated in the previous chapters. You will not see Gmail, the Play Store, or any other Google-made app on the Kindle Fire.

In this chapter, you will learn how to use the Amazon apps as replacements for the Google counterparts. We will begin with the most critical replacement: the Amazon App Store.

Using the Amazon App Store

Amazon was able to completely separate the Android operating system from the Google services that make the platform so popular by replacing them with comparable services that Amazon controls. The most important of these services for Amazon is the Play Store. Amazon replaced the Play Store with its own and provided the tools necessary for developers to easily release their apps on both the Google Play Store and Amazon's offering. Now, the Amazon App Store is available on every Android tablet, and it comes preloaded on the Kindle Fire.

Amazon offers a competitive service to the Play Store with its free app of the day. Every day Amazon takes an app that you would normally pay for and offers it for free on the Amazon App Store. Once you have installed the app, you have it for free for life.

If you're not a Fire owner, you need to install the App Store.

Installing the Amazon App Store

If you do not have a Kindle Fire, you will need to do a few things in order to install the Amazon App Store. Because the Amazon App Store is not something that can be installed via the Android Market, you must install it manually.

From your home screen, open the app drawer and select the Settings app. Inside Settings, locate the Applications tab and tap once. In the list of available options, you will see an "Unknown sources" option. Tapping the box next to this option will allow you to install apps without using the Play Store. Once you have tapped this check box, press the Home icon to be taken back to the home screen.

Open the app drawer and select the Browser app. When the browser loads, tap the URL bar at the top and type www.amazon.com. When you tap Go, you will be taken to the Amazon web site. From here, you will see a Get Amazon Apps for Android icon. Tapping this icon will take you to the list of Amazon apps available for your device. On this list you will see the Amazon App Store. Tap the App Store icon to begin downloading the app.

When the download has completed, you will see the following message appear in your notification tray: "Amazon_Appstore-release.apk has finished downloading." Tap the notification pop-up to begin the installation process. The installation screen, like the one shown in Figure 13–1, will show you the permissions the Amazon App Store will need in order to be installed. Tap the Install button on the bottom-left corner of this pop-up. Once the installation has been completed, you will be able to open the app and begin using the Amazon App Store.

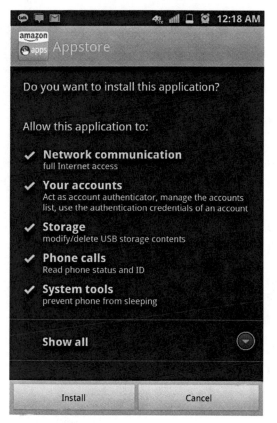

Figure 13–1. *Amazon App Store install screen*

Navigating the App Store

The first thing you see when you enter the Appstore is the free app of the day. Every day this space at the top of the Appstore screen will display a different app. You are shown a series of screenshots of the app, as well as the previously listed price for the app. The app might be productivity oriented or fitness oriented, or it might be a game. The app is chosen based on an agreement between the developer of the app and Amazon, and you will receive updates to the app as though you had purchased it.

As shown in Figure 13–2, beneath the free app of the day is a navigation bar for the different genres of apps. Slide your finger across the bar to reveal more genres. Beneath the navigation bar, Amazon has the top 100 and paid apps currently in its App Store. These apps are rated based on how many installations the app has had. Slide your finger from the bottom of the screen toward the top of the screen to see more of the 100 apps in both categories. If you already know which app you are looking for or if you are looking for a specific kind of app, the search bar at the top of the app will search the Appstore. Once you have located an app you are interested in, tap the icon for that app to be taken to the expanded view of that app.

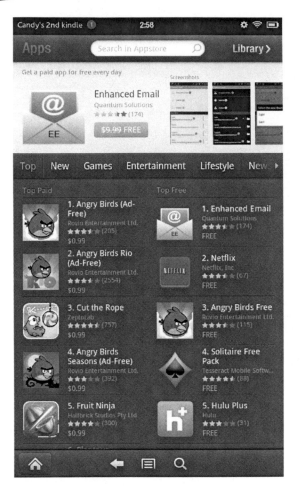

Figure 13–2. *Amazon App Store main view*

The expanded view for an app offers all of information Amazon has about it, as though you were looking at the app from its web site. From here, you can see what permissions the app would ask you for if you were to install it, including screenshots of the app in action, reviews of the app written by Amazon customers, and recommendations for other apps that were installed by users who installed this app. At the top of this view, the app is rated, out of five stars. This rating is a combination of all of the ratings the app has ever received. As shown in Figure 13–3, next to the stars, in parentheses, you will see how many people have rated the app.

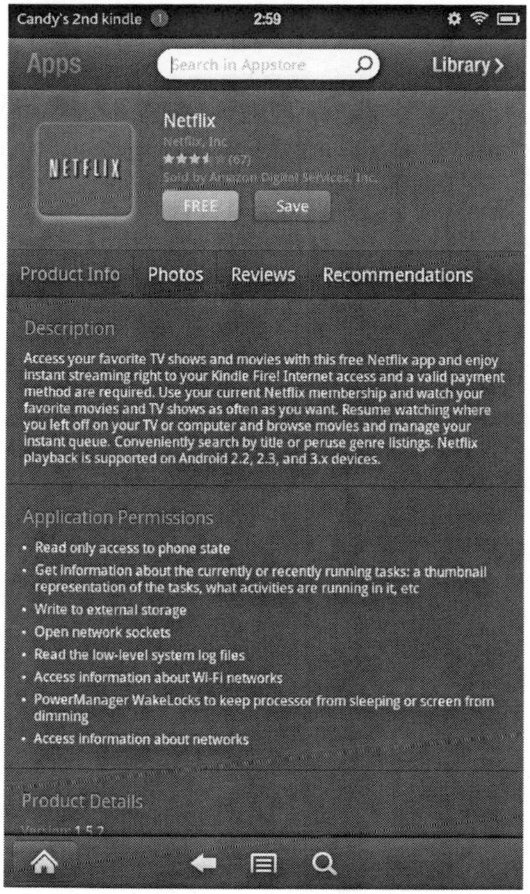

Figure 13–3. *Netflix app expanded view*

> **NOTE:** Pay attention to the ratings. An app that has five stars but has been rated only twice is not necessarily as good as an app that has four stars from more than 100 users. If an app is new, it may have only two ratings from people who helped the developer test his app.

Once you have decided to install the app, tap the gold icon at the top of the expanded view. If the app costs money, you will be directed to the Amazon checkout menu. Once the transaction is complete, the app will begin installation. Once installation is complete, Amazon Kindle Fire users will find the app in their Library, while other Android tablet users will find their new app in the app drawer.

Installing App Updates

When the developer of an app has released an update to the Amazon Appstore, you have the ability to install the update to the app whenever you are ready. When you open the Appstore on your tablet, you will receive a notification that there are updates available for you to install. If you are a Kindle Fire user, you will not get a notification. Instead, when you enter the Appstore and press the Menu key, you will see a red bubble next to the Updates icon with the number of apps that need to be updated in the bubble. If you are a Kindle Fire user, tap this bubble. Other Android tablets need only tap the notification when it pops up.

Apps that have updates available will appear in a list like the one in Figure 13–4. To install the update, tap the gold Install button next to the app. If the update to the app requires the use of any new permissions, you will be notified of them here. Tap each app to update it, and the app will remove itself from the list when it has finished installing.

Figure 13–4. *App updates for Amazon Appstore*

The Amazon Appstore offers a competitive service to the Play Store, unless you are using a Kindle Fire. The free app of the day is a great reason to keep the Amazon Appstore on your device and check it regularly.

One Amazon app that is always free is the Kindle e-book reader, which opens the world of Kindle e-books to any Android tablet owner. We'll look at that app in the next section.

Using the Kindle App

Originally, Amazon's digital book service was available to you only if you had an Amazon Kindle. Eventually, Amazon began to offer access to the Kindle library to other digital devices. Now, nearly any device with a screen and Internet access has the ability to display a Kindle book.

Installing the Kindle App

The Kindle app is available for every Android tablet and comes preloaded on the Kindle Fire. To install the Kindle app, search for the word *Kindle* in either the Android Market or the Amazon Appstore. When you find it, tap Install. Like all of Amazon's services, you require an Amazon account to access the app, but if you do not have one, it's easy enough to create one from the Kindle app.

The Kindle app includes access to the Amazon library of books, magazines, newspapers, and more. The Kindle library allows you to purchase books and to subscribe to magazines and newspapers such as those shown in Figure 13–5. From the Kindle app, tap the Store icon in the top right of the screen to access the Kindle bookstore and the Kindle Newsstand.

Figure 13–5. *Amazon Kindle Newsstand*

The Amazon library is organized by genre and includes a current list of best sellers in the Amazon bookstore underneath the navigation bar. At the top of the app is a search bar that allows you to search for specific titles or topics. Once you have chosen a book or magazine, you will be asked to purchase the item through the Amazon checkout. When the purchase is complete, your Kindle title will appear in the Library.

Reading in the Kindle App

Once you have an item in your Library, you can choose to "stream" the book to your tablet by downloading only a few chapters, or you can download the entire book. To download the book, press your finger to the book and hold it until a menu appears. Select "download to Home" from the list, and the book will begin downloading. Now, even if you are not connected to the Internet, you will have access to the book.

Whether you have decided to download the book or access chapters that are streamed to the tablet, the Kindle app keeps track of where you are in your book through software Amazon calls Whispersync. When you leave the Kindle app, Amazon stores your place in the book you were reading. When you are connected to the Internet, the Kindle app shares this information with your Amazon account. Now, if you were to access your Kindle books from your computer or from another device, the book would immediately go to where you left off. When inside a book, you can tap the screen and be shown your progress in the book, as shown in Figure 13–6.

Figure 13–6. *Kindle Whispersync*

The Kindle app takes up far less space than a physical library and allows you to store many more books, magazines, and newspapers than most people have room for. The ability to view everything the Kindle offers on your tablet and your computer makes it very easy to access your books anywhere you are.

Using the Amazon Video Store

Each of the Amazon apps on the Kindle Fire (except the Amazon Video app) has a counterpart that can be installed on any other Android tablet. This app gives users access to the Amazon digital video library. From this app, users can purchase movies and TV shows and either stream the video from Amazon.com or download the video to the Kindle Fire. If you are an Amazon Prime subscriber, many of the videos in the Amazon library are free to stream to your Kindle Fire.

From the home screen of the Kindle Fire, tap the Video tab to be taken to the Video store. The primary view of the Video store is broken down into three sections. The Prime Instant Videos section is a collection of free videos that can be streamed to your Kindle Fire if you have an Amazon Prime account. Beneath that, the Movies and TV Shows tabs in Figure 13–7 offer a selection of videos that are available both to rent and to purchase. From each of these sections, you can take your finger and slide from right to left to scroll through videos that are offered. If you would like to see more from a section, tap "View all" to be taken to a category view of that section. Each section allows you to browse the video collection by genre or by using the search at the top of the app. When you see a video you would like to learn more about, tap the image for the video.

Figure 13–7. *Amazon Video app on Kindle Fire*

From the expanded view of any video, you have access to a significant amount of information. If you are looking at a movie, like the one shown in Figure 13–8, you can watch the trailer for the movie from the app. You can read a movie synopsis or tap Movie Details and see who starred in the movie. If you are looking for a similar movie, the bottom of the page has a selection of movies that other customers who watched this video also considered.

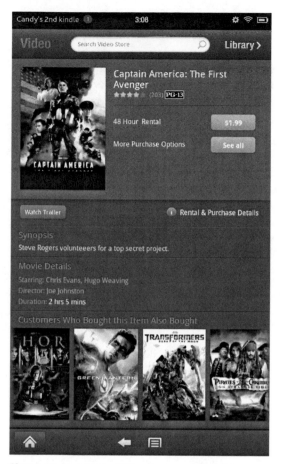

Figure 13–8. *Amazon Video store expanded view*

If you've decided to watch this video, you have the option to rent or buy the movie. If you rent the movie, it will be available in your Library for 48 hours, and then the movie will remove itself. If you choose to buy the movie, you will have the ability to either download the movie or stream it from Amazon. If you download the movie, you will not need an Internet connection to watch it.

The Amazon Video store is growing daily, and the movies that you buy there are always available to you as long as you have an Internet connection. The videos are available in many places, not just your Kindle Fire. Any computer with a web browser can access the videos from your Amazon account, and many Blu-ray players and "smart TVs" now offer the Amazon video library, giving you the ability to watch your digital videos almost anywhere.

Summary

Amazon has taken its massive digital library and turned it into a series of apps that allow you to carry your favorite books, movies, TV shows, and games with you anywhere. The only limitation is how much storage you have on your device (if you're not connected to the Internet all the time).

I thank you for taking the time to read Taking Your Android Tablet to the Max. It is my deepest with that the information held within these pages helps you be not only enjoy your Tablet, but feel confident in your use of it. I hope you share the knowledge you gained from this book with everyone else you know who is considering a Tablet. Every day there are more new things to do with your Tablet. New apps are being written, and with that brings new features and new possibilities. Whether your Tablet is a replacement for your laptop, a fun new gadget for the living room, or just a way for you to read books on the go, I hope that this book has been helpful.

Index

A

Accounts & Sync, 122
Additional ports, in tablet, 34
Adobe Photoshop Express app, 96, 97
ADW Launcher, 160, 164
 Honeycomb, resetting defaults in, 165
 Honeycomb, selection screen in, 161
ADW Launcher EX, 160
 on Honeycomb, 162
 Settings menu, 163
Amazon
 App Store, 17
 movies and music, 17
 Silk browser, 17
Amazon App Store, 177
 installation, 178–179
 navigation
  expanded view, 180–181
  main view, 179–180
 updates installation, 182–183
Amazon Kindle Fire, 17–18
Amazon Video Store
 expanded view, 186–187
 Kindle Fire, 186
Android
 history
  Google Nexus One, 6–7
  iPad, 7–8
  Motorola Droid, 5–6
  Open Handset Alliance, 2–4
  T-Mobile G1, 5
 tablet (see Android tablet)
 user interface options, 12
  Amazon Kindle Fire, 17–18

  Android, 23
  Android 4.0, 21–22
  HTC Sense, 13–15
  Samsung TouchWiz, 16–17
  Stock Android 3.0 (Honeycomb), 18–21
Android 3.0 (Honeycomb), 18–21
Android 4.0, 21–22
Android apps
 choice of, 73–75
 installation, 75–76
 review submission, 78
 updation, 77
Android Camera apps, 89
Android, Inc., 2, 12
Android Market home page, 71
Android Open Source Project, 3, 13, 15
Android OS, 49
 advantages of, 25
Android tablet, 1, 8–12, 121–132, 155–165
 augmented reality
  Google Sky Map, 128–130
  Layar, 130–132
 camera
  photograph, 92, 93
  settings, 90–91
  video recording, 92, 93
 Dropbox, files storage in Cloud, 126–128
 home screen customization, 160–165
 Internet access, 10
  4G service, 12
  Wi-Fi/3G/4G, 11

keyboard customization
    handwritten and voice input,
      158–160
    Thumb Keyboard, 155–158
listening to music, 99
    doubleTwist app and
      doubleTwist AirSync app,
      105–109
    playing stored music, 100–105
playing games
    Google Market, 117–118
    Nvidia Tegra Zone, 118–119
    USB controller, 119–120
rooting (see Rooted tablet)
screen size
    7-inch tablets, 10
    8- to 10-inch tablets, 10
    less than 7-inch, 10
screen type, 9
watching stored movies, 110–111
watching streamed movies
    Google Videos, renting, 111–115
    Netflix app, 115–116
    viewing tablet videos on TV, 116
with Google Chrome, 122–123
with phone, 123–126
Andy, 4
Angry Birds, 117
Apple iPad, 7–8
AT&T, 5, 7
Augmented reality
    Google Sky Map, 128–130
    Layar, 130–132

▨ B

BADA platform, 16
Bookworm, tablet user, 28–29
Bootloader, 4
Browser, Google account creation from,
    41, 42
Bugdroid, 4

▨ C

Camcorder function, in Camera app, 92

Camera
    Android Camera apps, 89
    Android tablet camera
      photograph, 92, 93
      settings, 90–91
      video recording, 92, 93
    Gallery app
      Grid view, 93–94
      single-item view, 94–95
    on mobile devices, 89
    Paper Camera app, 95–97
    settings, 91
    on tablets, 26
Camera app, 89, 90
Capacitive touchscreen, 9
Certificate protection, with password,
    141–142
Charging, tablet, 33
Chrome to Phone, 123–126
Chrome to Phone Extension link, 123
Chrome sync setup form on computer,
    122
Cloud
    computing with, 148
      Google Goggles, searching for
        images with, 149–151
      Opera Mini browser, internet
        browsing with, 153–154
      Wyse PocketCloud, home data
        storage assessment, 151–153
    data storage
      Google Docs, managing word
        documents with, 148
      with SugarSync, 145–148
Cloud-based storage system, 126
Cloud computing, 80, 145
Cloud, files storage in, with Dropbox,
    126–128
Cloud (Google), 11
Coldplay, in Google Music shop, 88
Color effect, 91
Computing with Cloud
    Google Goggles, searching for
      images with, 149–151
    Opera Mini browser, internet
      browsing with, 153–154

Wyse PocketCloud, home data
storage assessment, 151–153
Contacts, in Google account, 44
adding contacts manually, 46–48
importing, 45–46
Customizing Gmail, 53–55

D

Data storage, in Cloud
Google Docs, managing word
documents with, 148
with SugarSync, 145–148
Dell Streak, 10
Device administration, 142–143
Digital zoom, 91
DLNA technology, 116
doubleTwist AirSync app, 105–109
Dropbox, 145
Dropbox, files storage in Cloud,
126–128

E

eBay, 2
E-mail, composing, 51–53
E-mail view, in Gmail, 51
Empowering system administrator,
142–143
Encrypting stored information, in Tablet,
139–140
Encrypt tablet view, in Honeycomb,
139–140
Exploring files, with Terminal app,
169–170

F

Facebook, 15, 17, 122
Flash, 154
Flash mode, 91
Flex T9 keyboard, 155, 158, 159
Fluxed ADW theme, 164
Fragmentation, 22
Front-facing camera, 26, 89

G

Gallery app, 89, 90
Grid view, 93–94
single-item view, 94–95
Games, on Android tablet, 120
Google Market, 117–118
Nvidia Tegra Zone, 118–119
Gmail, 49
for Android 3.1 E-mail view, 51
for Android 3.0 Inbox view, 50
customizing, 53–55
E-mail, composing, 51–53
navigation
E-mail view, 51
Inbox view, 50
Google account creation
from browser, 41, 42
contacts, 44
adding contacts manually, 46–48
importing, 45–46
on Google.com, 40–42
Google.com sign-in, 38
with Honeycomb, 39, 40
Honeycomb sign-in, 38
syncing with Google account, 42–44
from tablet, 38–40
Google Account, in Tablet, 136–139
Google Apps
Gmail, 49–55
Google Maps, 59–64
Google Talk, 55–59
search, 67–69
YouTube, 64–67
Google Authenticator, 138, 139
Google Books, in Android Market,
80–83
Google Checkout, 75, 88
Google Chrome, 20
Google.com
account on, 40–42
sign-in, 38
Google Docs, 148
Google Goggles, searching for images
with, 149–151
Google Latitude, 63–64

Google Maps, 20, 59
  on Android 3.1, 60
  driving directions in, 62–63
  Driving Navigation, 63
  layers in, 60–62
  locating friends with latitude, 63–64
  Search Maps, 60
Google Market games, 117–118
Google Movies
  in Android Market, 83–86
  shop, 84
Google Music, 148
  in Android Market, 86–88
  Carousel view, 101, 102
  list view, 103
  sorting menu, 104
Google Nexus One, 6–7
Google's cloud, 11
Google Sky Map, 128–130
Google's two-step verification, 136
Google Talk, 44, 55
  adding some friends, 56
  chatting with a friend, 57
  customizing settings, 58–59
  setting status message, 57
  video chatting with a friend, 57–58
Google Videos, renting, 111–115
Google Web Market interface, 80
Grid view, Gallery app, 93–94
3G service, 11
4G service, 12

H

Handwritten and voice input, 158–160
HDMI port, 34
Home data storage assessment, with
    Wyse PocketCloud, 151–153
Home screen customization, 160–165
Honeycomb
  ADW Launcher EX on, 162
  ADW Launcher selection screen in,
    161
  configuring lock screen in, 134
  credential storage view in, 141
  encrypt tablet view in, 140
  Google account with, 39, 40
  Google Authenticator app in, 139
  Google Docs home screen on, 148
  Google Goggles image scan in, 150
  keyboard settings in, 156
  Movies app for, 112
  Netflix app on, 116
  new contact, adding, 48
  Opera Mini Browser start screen in,
    154
  owner info screen in, 135
  password-protect credentials in, 142
  pattern lock screen with owner info
    in, 136
  QRCode scanning Google Goggles
    for, 150
  resetting ADW Launcher defaults in,
    165
  sign-in, 38
  SugarSync
    file manager on, 146, 147
    main menu on, 146, 147
    setup screen, 146
  syncing your Google apps with, 44
  Tegra Zone on, 119
  Terminal app, 169
  USB controller, 120
  Wyse PocketCloud
    autodiscovery screen in, 152
    desktop view in, 153
Honeycomb Android Market
  app view, 74
  Category view in, 73
  credit card details, 76
  home page, 72
  My Apps view, 77
  purchasing app, 75
Honeycomb app, purchasing movies
    with, 113
Honeycomb Camera app, 90
Honeycomb home screen, music player
    on, 105
Honeycomb tablets, Screenshot app,
    174, 175
Honeycomb Videos app, Personal
    Videos tab of, 111

HSPA+ technology, 12
HTC, 2
HTC Flyer Android tablet, 14
HTC Sense, 13–15
Hulu, 115–116

I, J

Importing contacts, 45–46
Inbox view, in Gmail, 50
Intel, 2
Internet
    mobile Internet 3G/4G contract
        mobile hotspot, 27
        tethering, 27
    Pay-as-you-go mobile Internet
        3G/4G, 27
    Wi-Fi only, 27
Internet access, in Android tablet, 10
    4G service, 12
    Wi-Fi/3G/4G, 11
Internet browsing, speeding up, Opera
    Mini browser, 153–154
iPad, 7–8

K

Keyboard customization
    handwritten and voice input,
        158–160
    Honeycomb, keyboard settings in,
        156
    Thumb Keyboard, 155–158
Kindle App, 183–184
Kindle Fire, 177, 186
Kindle Whispersync, 184–185

L

Layar
    Popular layers view, 130, 131
    Yelp layer view, 131, 132
LCD display, 9
Linux operating system, 167, 169
Locking screen, in Tablet, 133–134
Long Term Evolution (LTE), 12

LucasFilm, 6

M

Magnetic strips, 34
Memory, in tablet
    onboard memory, 26
    removable storage, 26
MicroSD card, 26, 141
Mini HDMI port, 34
Mobile hotspot, 27
Mobile Internet 3G/4G contract
    mobile hotspot, 27
    tethering, 27
Mobile office user, 29
Motorola, 2, 20
Motorola Cliq, 5
Motorola Droid, 5–6
Movie purchase, detailed view of, 114
Movies, on Android tablet
    watching stored movies, 110–111
    watching streamed movies
        Google Videos, renting, 111–115
        Netflix app, 115–116
        TV, videos on, 116
Movies app, with purchased movie, 115
Music and movie junkie, tablet user, 28
Music, on Android tablet, 99
    doubleTwist app and doubleTwist
        AirSync app, 105–109
    playing stored music, 100–105
My Apps, 50
MySpace, 15, 17

N

Netflix app, 115–116
Nexus One *vs.* Nexus S, 6
nVidia, 2
Nvidia Tegra Zone games, 118–119

O

OHA. *See* Open Handset Alliance
OLED display, 9
Onboard memory, 26

Open Handset Alliance (OHA), 2–5
Open source, 3
Opera Mini browser
    Honeycomb, start screen in, 154
    speeding up internet browsing with,
        153–154
Owner information, in Tablet, 135–136

P

PacketVideo, 2
Paper Camera app, 95–97
Pay-as-you-go mobile Internet 3G/4G,
    27
Phone, Android tablet, 123–126
Photograph, 92, 93
Pixel Qi display, 9
Play Store
    Android apps, 71–72
        choice of, 73–75
        installation, 75–76
        review submission, 78
        updation, 77
    Google Books, 80–83
    Google Movies, 83–86
    Google Music, 86–88
    from web browser, 79–80
PocketCloud. See Wyse PocketCloud
Proprietary network connections
    protecting certificate with password,
        141–142
    security certificate, 140–141

Q

QRCode, 149, 150

R

Rear-facing camera, 26, 93
Remote administration, 142
Removable storage, 26
Resistive touchscreen, 9
Road warrior, tablet user, 27
Rom Manager, for Android, 171

Rooted tablet
    backing up data, 170
        Rom Manager, 171
        Titanium Backup, 172–173
    exploring files, with Terminal app,
        169–170
    permission, 167–168
    screenshot, 173–175
Root File Explorer, 170
Rooting, 154
RootzWiki.com, 168
Rotating camera, 26
Rubin, Andy, 12

S

Samsung, 16
Samsung Galaxy Note, 10
Samsung Galaxy Tab, 9
Samsung TouchWiz, 16–17
Scene mode, 91
Screenshot, in Android Market,
    173–175
Screen size, of tablet, 25
Secondary cameras, 89
Security certificate installation, 140–141
Security credential, 140
SenseUI, 16, 17
SIM card, 34–35
Single-item view, Gallery app, 94–95
Slacker Radio, 109
Snakes game, 117
SoundHound app, 109
Sprint, 2, 5, 12
SprintID service, 13
Stock Android 3.0 (Honeycomb), 18–21
Stock keyboard, 155
Student/teacher, tablet user, 28
SugarSync
    data storage with, 145–148
    Honeycomb
        file manager on, 146, 147
        main menu on, 146, 147
        setup screen with, 145
Switching cameras, 91
Sync browser, 122

T

Tablet
  empowering system administrator, 142–143
  encrypting stored information, 139–140
  features
    cameras, 26
    Internet, 27
    memory, 26
    size, 25
  Google account from, 38–40
  place of purchase
    accessories, 30–31
    carrier stores, 29
    electronics stores, 29
    warehouse stores, 29
    warranty/insurance, 30
  proprietary network connections
    protecting certificate with password, 141–142
    security certificate, 140–141
  searching
    with keypad, 68
    with spoken words, 68–69
  securing
    Google Account, 136–139
    locking screen, 133–134
    owner information, 135–136
  setting up, 32
    additional ports, 34
    first charge, 33
    powering up, 35
    SIM card, 34–35
  Thumb Keyboard for, 158
  unboxing, 31
    PC dock, 32
    separate power cord and USB cable, 32
    single removable cable, 32
  user, kind of
    bookworm, 28–29
    mobile office user, 29
    music and movie junkie, 28
    road warrior, 27
    student/teacher, 28

tech gearhead, 28
Tech gearhead, tablet user, 28
Terminal app, exploring files with, 169–170
Tethering, 27
Thumb Keyboard, 155
  Honeycomb, keyboard settings in, 156
  input select screen with multiple keyboards, 157
  for tablets, 158
Titanium Backup, 172–173
T-Mobile, 2
T-Mobile G1, 5
TouchWiz (Samsung), 16–17
Twitter, 15, 17
Two-step verification (Google), 136–138

U

Unboxing tablet, 31–32
USB controller, 119–120

V

VCast service (Verizon), 13
Verizon, 5, 13
Video quality, 92
Video recording, 92, 93
Virtual keyboard, 155
Virtual private networks (VPNs), 140
Voice search, in Android 3.1, 69
Voice translation on Flex T9 keyboard, 160
VPNs. *See* Virtual private networks

W

Web browser, Android Market from, 79–80
White balance, 91
Wi-Fi, 11
Wi-Fi only, 27
WiMax, 12
Word documents management, with Google Docs, 148

Wyse PocketCloud
    home data storage assessment,
        151–153
    Honeycomb
        autodiscovery screen in, 152
        desktop view in, 153

X

XDA-Developers, 168

Y, Z

Yelp, 130, 131
YouTube, 64
    check out the Wall, 65–66
    sharing videos, 67
    storing videos, 66

CPSIA information can be obtained at www.ICGtesting.com
Printed in the USA
LVOW051438180412

278182LV00001B/2/P